BCBR Made Simple

A Student-Friendly Guide to Basics of Biomedical Research

Dr Javed Ali

First Edition — 2026

Dedicated to my wife, Saba.

Disclaimer

Introduction: Why Research Matters

Imagine you are a doctor in a small town. A cluster of patients arrives with a strange illness you have never seen before. How do you figure out what is causing it? How do you know which treatment will work? How do you convince the health ministry to act? The answer to all three questions is the same: research.

Biomedical research is not some abstract activity reserved for people in white lab coats staring at test tubes. It is the engine that drives every clinical decision, every public health policy, and every new drug on the pharmacy shelf. Without it, medicine would still be bloodletting and prayer.

This book “BCBR Made Simple “is your guide to the Basics of Biomedical Research. It is written for students, clinicians, and early-career researchers who want to understand how health research actually works: from asking the right question, all the way to writing a grant proposal and publishing your findings.

The book organizes the topics into 14 logical chapters. Each chapter has plain-language explanations, comparison tables, memory aids, highlight boxes, and exam insights drawn from actual exam questions. By the end, you will not just know the content you will understand it.

This book focuses on exam-favourite concepts and key takeaways to help students perform better in exams. Throughout each chapter, you will find specially designed learning elements including:

- **High-Yield Points to Remember** — concise summaries of the most tested and most important facts in each topic.
- **Exam Insights** — targeted guidance drawn from the pattern of questions that appear in competitive and university examinations.

These elements are designed to reinforce understanding, sharpen exam readiness, and help you recall what matters most when it counts.

Table of Contents

Chapter 1: Foundations of Health Research: What Exactly Are We Doing and Why Are We Doing It?

In 1854, London was gripped by a devastating cholera outbreak. The prevailing theory blamed 'bad air'. A physician named John Snow decided to actually investigate. He mapped every death and traced them all to a single water pump on Broad Street. He removed the pump handle. The outbreak stopped. That was early epidemiology — and it saved thousands of lives. That is what health research does.

1.1 The Many Dimensions of Health Research

Health research spans a vast spectrum — from the molecular to the population level, from purely theoretical to intensely practical. Think of it as a relay race: different researchers hand the baton from one stage to the next until a laboratory discovery becomes a life-saving tool.

Table 1.1: Dimensions of Health Research

Dimension	What It Does	Real-World Example
Theoretical	Builds the knowledge base; basic science	Mapping the full genome of Hepatitis B virus
Applied	Uses theoretical knowledge in practice	Developing a vaccine from genomic data
Preventive	Tests preventive technologies	INH prophylaxis to prevent TB in HIV patients
Therapeutic	Tests new treatments and drugs	Injectable iron for pregnancy anaemia
Implementation	Improves programme delivery and scale-up	Evaluating the IDSP for epidemic prediction capacity
Translational	Bench to bedside — converts lab findings to human benefit	Applying lab findings directly to patient welfare

High-Yield: Remember This!

- Bench-to-bedside = Translational Research. This is a favourite exam question.
- The dimensions form a relay race: Theoretical → Applied → Preventive/Therapeutic → Implementation.
- No dimension is 'better' than another — each serves a distinct purpose.

1.2 Types of Research: A Full Taxonomy

Research can be categorised along several axes. Understanding these will help you both in study design and in answering exam questions with precision.

Table 1.2: Types of Research

Type	Key Feature	Example
Exploratory	No prior knowledge; finding initial clues	First investigation of a brand-new disease outbreak
Confirmatory	Strengthens or tests existing evidence	Verifying risk factors found in a pilot study
Qualitative	Open-ended; interviews; focus group discussions	Community perceptions of vaccination hesitancy

Quantitative	Structured questionnaires; numerical data	Seroprevalence surveys
Observational	Investigator does NOT change the environment	Cross-sectional, cohort, case-control studies
Experimental	Investigator assigns the intervention	Randomised Controlled Trials (RCTs)
Retrospective	Outcome has already occurred at study start	Historical cohort using past employment records
Prospective	Follows disease-free participants forward in time	The Framingham Heart Study

1.3 The Three Levels of Review

Every legitimate research project must pass through three distinct review processes before a single participant is enrolled. Think of these as three bouncers at the door of the research club — each checking a different part of your ID.

- **Scientific Review:** Evaluates the novelty, rationality, and justification of your research concept. Is the question worth asking? Is the method sound?
- **Ethics Review:** Ensures human participants are protected from physical, psychological, and social harm.
- **Regulatory Review:** Reviews foreign funding, biological sample shipments, intellectual property rights, and international collaborations. Protects national interests.

Common Exam Confusion

- Ethics review protects HUMAN PARTICIPANTS.
- Regulatory review protects INTELLECTUAL PROPERTY and national interests.
- They are NOT the same thing!

1.4 Objectives of Health Research

Research is never done for its own sake — it must have a purpose. The recognised objectives include:

- Creating entirely new information — for example, discovering the complete genome structure of Hepatitis E virus.
- Obtaining additional information on existing problems — for example, studying diphtheria in adults, where data was previously only available for children.
- Verifying and confirming existing information — for example, checking whether the known causes of paediatric pneumonia hold true across countries.
- Finding cause-and-effect relationships — for example, investigating the link between breast implants and breast cancer risk.

- Testing new interventions — drugs, vaccines, screening tools, and preventive technologies.
- Evaluating ongoing government programmes — for example, assessing whether a national disease surveillance system can predict epidemics.

1.5 Critical Planning Considerations

A well-designed study does not just happen. Skipping planning steps is like building a house on sand — everything looks fine until the first storm.

- Adequate justification and rationale for why the study is worth doing.
- A clear, focused research question — one issue, stated unambiguously.
- Standard, unambiguous case definitions for all study variables.
- A qualitatively representative sample to ensure external validity and generalisability.
- Adequate sample size to ensure sufficient statistical power.
- A pilot study — a rehearsal run to identify practical difficulties before the main study begins.
- Well-defined inclusion and exclusion criteria.
- Standardised data collection instruments.
- A statistical analysis plan decided at the outset — before data collection begins.
- Proper laboratory controls (positive and negative) and external quality assurance.

1.6 Errors in Research

Error Type	Definition	How to Minimise
Random Error	Natural biological variation between individuals; not systematic; unpredictable	Increase sample size
Bias (Systematic Error)	Distortion from faulty procedure, measurement, or enrollment — consistently skews results in one direction	Improve study design; use rigorous standardised protocols

1.7 Confounders and Effect Modifiers

These two concepts trip up more students than almost anything else in research methods. A confounder is a third-wheel variable that is independently associated with BOTH your exposure AND your outcome. It creates a false impression of causation. Classic example: coffee drinking appears to cause lung cancer — until you realise that coffee drinkers also tend to smoke, and smoking is the real culprit. Smoking is the confounder.

An effect modifier, by contrast, genuinely changes the true relationship between exposure and outcome in different subgroups. It does not confuse things — it reveals that the effect is different in different groups.

Table 1.3: Confounders vs. Effect Modifiers

Concept	Definition	How to Handle
Confounder	Independently associated with BOTH the exposure AND the outcome; not on the causal pathway	Collect data on all known confounders; control using statistical analysis (stratification, regression)
Effect Modifier	Independently alters the true exposure-outcome relationship in different subgroups	Be aware of it; consider analysing and reporting results separately by subgroup

Key Takeaways — Chapter 1

- Health research spans six dimensions. Translational = bench to bedside.
- Three types of review: Scientific (novelty), Ethics (human protection), Regulatory (IP and national interests).
- Random error is reduced by increasing sample size. Bias is reduced by better study design.
- Confounders require statistical control. Effect modifiers require subgroup analysis.
- A pilot study is a rehearsal — it identifies practical difficulties before the real study begins.

Chapter 2: Asking the Right Question: How to Stop Wandering in Circles and Actually Get Somewhere

Einstein reportedly said that if he had one hour to save the world, he would spend 55 minutes defining the problem and only 5 minutes solving it. In research, the same logic applies. A poorly framed research question is the single most common reason studies fail, findings are unpublishable, and researchers end up staring at a wall wondering where it all went wrong.

2.1 The Research Life Cycle

Research is not a straight line — it is a cycle. Each completed study generates new knowledge that raises new questions, which trigger the next round of research.

Table 2.1: The Research Life Cycle

Step	What Happens
1	Uncertainty / Data Need — something is unknown and needs an answer
2	Research Question — the uncertainty is framed as a specific, answerable question
3	Study Objectives + Analysis Plan — the question is broken into measurable objectives

4	Data Collection Instruments — questionnaires, forms, and tools are designed
5	Data Collection — information is gathered from the study population
6	Analysis — data is processed and patterns are identified
7	Conclusions + Recommendations — findings are interpreted and acted upon
8	Share with Stakeholders — results communicated to those who can act on them, triggering the next cycle

2.2 What Is a Research Question?

A research question is an uncertainty about something in the population that the investigator wants to resolve by making measurements in the study population. Notice the key words: uncertainty (you do not already know the answer), measurements (it must be empirically testable), and population (it applies to a group, not just one patient).

A good research question must:

- Focus on ONE issue — not three questions disguised as one.
- Be written in everyday language — no jargon-filled sentences that need a decoder ring.
- Link to an actionable outcome — the answer must be useful for something.
- Be stated as a question — obviously, but you would be surprised how many 'research questions' are actually statements.

2.3 Categories of Research Questions

Table 2.2: Categories of Research Questions

Type	Features	Key Question Words	Example
Descriptive	Measures a quantity; no comparison group; no intervention	How many? How much? What is the extent?	What is the prevalence of physical inactivity among diabetic patients?
Analytical	Has a comparison group OR tests a hypothesis	Greater/less than, causes, leads to, associated with, compared with	Does brisk walking for 1 hour per day reduce fasting blood sugar in type 2 diabetics compared to non-walkers?

2.4 Sources of Research Ideas

Research ideas do not fall from the sky. They come from systematic effort:

- **Literature scholarship** — up-to-date reading reveals gaps and contradictions that need investigation.
- **New ideas and techniques** — conferences, new technology applied to old problems, a sceptical attitude towards accepted wisdom.

- **Clinical and laboratory observations** — everyday practice often raises questions that no study has yet answered.
- **Tenacity and mentorship** — a good supervisor helps a trainee frame a vague curiosity into a rigorous research question.

2.5 Six Steps to Conceive a Research Question

Here is a systematic process for transforming a fuzzy idea into a focused, rigorous question, using the example of exercise and diabetes:

Table 2.3: Six Steps to Formulate a Research Question

Step	Action	Diabetes Example
1	Review the state-of-the-art literature	Exercise reduces blood sugar and body fat — this is established.
2	Raise an initial question	'Can exercise help control blood sugar level?'
3	Peer review — is it worth investigating?	Consult experts; decide if the question is novel and feasible enough.
4	Define measurable exposures and outcomes	Exercise = 60 min brisk walking daily; Outcome = Fasting Blood Sugar level
5	Sharpen the question	'Does 1 hour of daily physical activity reduce fasting blood sugar in diabetics?'
6	Specify all details	Include study population, operational definitions, and design type.

2.6 The FINER Test

Before committing to a research question, run it through the FINER test. If it fails any criterion, fix the question or find a different one.

Table 2.4: The FINER Criteria

Letter	Criterion	Key Questions to Ask
F	Feasible	Do you have enough participants? The technical expertise? Sufficient time and money?
I	Interesting	Does it enthuse you and your colleagues? Is it genuinely worth doing?
N	Novel	Does it confirm, refute, or extend existing findings? Is it genuinely new information?
E	Ethical	Will the ethics committee approve it? Will it harm or exploit participants?
R	Relevant	Will it advance science, improve clinical practice, or inform health policy?

2.7 The Research Hypothesis

A hypothesis is the supercharged version of the research question. It is a specific, testable statement that summarises the main elements of the study — the sample, exposures, and outcomes — and provides the foundation for statistical testing.

One important rule: hypotheses are generally required for analytical studies — ones that compare two or more groups. Descriptive studies, which simply measure a quantity, do not need a hypothesis.

A good hypothesis must be:

- **Simple** — one exposure, one outcome. No multiple-choice hypotheses.
- **Specific** — no ambiguity about who the participants are or what is being measured.
- **A priori** — stated before data collection begins, not after you have seen the results (that is called data dredging and it destroys your study's credibility).
- **Focused** — centred around the primary objective.

2.8 Study Objectives

Study objectives translate the research question into specific, measurable actions. They tell the reader exactly what you are going to do.

Feature	Descriptive Objective	Analytical Objective
Purpose	Estimate a quantity by observation	Test a hypothesis by comparing two or more groups
Preferred Verb	'To estimate'	'To determine'
Comparison Group?	No	Yes
Example	Estimate the prevalence of physical inactivity among diabetic patients	Determine the effect of brisk walking (1 hr/day) on fasting blood sugar in type 2 diabetics compared to non-walkers

Exam Insights

- Hypotheses are generally required for analytical questions (those with comparison groups).
- Good hypothesis: Simple (1 exposure, 1 outcome), Specific, A priori (pre-specified before data collection).
- Descriptive objective verb = 'To estimate'. Analytical objective verb = 'To determine'.
- Avoid using 'to study' as the verb in a study objective — it is too vague and not recommended.
- FINER = Feasible, Interesting, Novel, Ethical, Relevant.

Key Takeaways — Chapter 2

- A research question is an uncertainty about the population resolved by measurements.
- Descriptive questions ask 'How much?' Analytical questions ask 'What causes?' or 'What is the effect?'
- Use the FINER test to evaluate every research question before committing.
- Hypotheses are only for analytical questions; must be stated before data collection begins.
- Preferred verbs: 'Estimate' for descriptive objectives; 'Determine' for analytical objectives.

Chapter 3: Standing on Others' Shoulders — The Literature Review: How to Avoid Reinventing the Wheel and Other Research Disasters

> *Isaac Newton wrote: 'If I have seen further, it is by standing on the shoulders of giants.' Before you can see further, you need to know exactly where the giants currently stand. That is the purpose of a literature review — not paperwork, but navigation.*

A good literature review answers some questions — and raises many more.

3.1 Why Conduct a Literature Review?

Some students treat the literature review as a bureaucratic formality — a box to tick before the 'real' research. This is a costly mistake. A thorough literature review:

- Provides the link between what is already known and what is not yet known.
- Saves enormous time — you may find a perfectly validated questionnaire already exists, saving months of development work.
- Helps you understand the subject far more deeply before you begin.
- Identifies gaps (lacunae) in existing knowledge — and these gaps are precisely where your research question lives.
- Aids in developing new research methods for an established subject area.

3.2 What a Literature Review Is — and Is Not

Table 3.1: What a Literature Review Is and Is Not

A Literature Review IS...	A Literature Review is NOT...
Organised, systematic information seeking	Just a summary of articles you happened to read
Critical appraisal of collected articles	Uncritical, passive reading of sources
Synthesis: identifying what is and is not known	A simple listing of study findings
Identification of gaps in knowledge (lacunae)	A fault-finding exercise to tear down other researchers
Scholarly analysis of strengths and weaknesses	Distortion or selective reporting of findings to suit your hypothesis

3.3 Where to Search

Not all sources are equal. Knowing which database to use for which purpose makes your searches far more efficient.

Table 3.2: Key Literature Search Databases

Resource	Type	Best For
PubMed / MEDLINE	Biomedical citations database (25M+ citations; free; maintained by NLM/NIH)	Peer-reviewed biomedical and clinical articles
Cochrane Library	Systematic reviews and meta-analyses	Highest level of evidence for clinical questions
Scopus / Google Scholar	Large multi-disciplinary citation databases	Broad literature searches across disciplines
PubMed Central (PMC)	Free full-text articles linked from PubMed	Open-access complete articles
HON-Certified Websites	Health on Net accredited websites	Reliable general health information
MeSH (NLM Vocabulary)	Controlled vocabulary thesaurus maintained by NLM	Precise, indexing-based searches in PubMed

High-Yield Facts

- PubMed: 25M+ biomedical citations; free; maintained by NLM/NIH.
- MeSH = Medical Subject Headings — the NLM's controlled vocabulary thesaurus.
- Cochrane Library = highest level of evidence (systematic reviews and meta-analyses).
- Vancouver and Harvard are the standard citation styles in biomedical research.

3.4 Boolean Search Logic: The Three Magic Words

Boolean operators are the power tools of literature searching. Used across all major databases, they let you expand, narrow, or refine your search with surgical precision. There are only three operators:

Table 3.3: Boolean Search Operators

Operator	Logic	Effect	Example (Lung + Infections)
AND	Both terms must be present	NARROWS the search — most specific	~82,000 articles specifically about lung infections
OR	Either or both terms present	BROADENS the search — most inclusive	~2.4 million articles (all lung OR all infection articles)
NOT	First term present, second absent	EXCLUDES a specific topic	~6.3 lakh articles on lung (excluding infections)

3.5 Steps in Conducting a Literature Review

Table 3.4: Steps in Conducting a Literature Review

Step	What to Do
1. Systematic Search	Use Boolean operators and MeSH terms in PubMed, Cochrane, and Scopus to collect all relevant articles.
2. Critical Appraisal	Apply scholarly (not fault-finding) judgment: assess validity, identify strengths, weaknesses, and knowledge gaps.
3. Compare Methods and Results	Understand the methodologies used across studies; identify patterns and inconsistencies.
4. Tabulate Findings	Organise each study in a table: Citation | Design | Objectives | Population | Sample Size | Outcomes | Main Findings | Authors' Conclusions. Arrange chronologically (recent to past).
5. Write the Review	Introduction, empirical literature summary with scholarly appraisal, and a concise conclusion summarising what is and is not known.

3.6 Writing the Literature Review

A well-written literature review has three sections:

- **Introduction:** State the purpose of the review, explain how it is organised, and the basis of ordering (e.g., chronological or thematic).
- **Empirical Literature:** Discuss quality studies in a positive, paraphrased form. Apply scholarly critical appraisal — acknowledge strengths, novel methods, and gaps. Never cherry-pick findings to support your hypothesis or distort results.
- **Summary:** A concise conclusion stating what is known, what is not known, and where the gaps lie. This summary directly justifies your research question.

3.7 Ethical Concerns in Literature Review

Even a literature review has ethical obligations that are often overlooked:

- Present content honestly — do not selectively report findings that support your hypothesis while ignoring contradictory evidence.
- Address study weaknesses in a scholarly manner — critique the methodology, not the authors personally. Scholarly means research-focused, not fault-finding.
- Cite all sources accurately using a standard citation style. Vancouver (numbered) and Harvard (author-date) are the most common in biomedical research.

Key Takeaways — Chapter 3

- A literature review identifies gaps (lacunae) in knowledge — the very foundation of new research.
- PubMed: 25M+ citations; free; NLM/NIH. MeSH = controlled vocabulary for precise searches.
- Boolean: AND narrows, OR broadens, NOT excludes.
- Critical appraisal = scholarly, not fault-finding.
- The summary section of the review directly justifies your research question.

Chapter 4: Counting Disease — Measures of Disease Frequency: How Epidemiologists Keep Score

If you want to fight a disease, you first need to know how common it is, how fast it is spreading, and how dangerous it is once you catch it. These three questions are answered by three distinct measures: prevalence, incidence, and case fatality. Master these, and you have the core language of epidemiology.

Epidemiology is about measuring disease — not judging outcomes.

4.1 Population at Risk

Before counting cases, you must define who is actually susceptible. The population at risk is the portion of the population that can develop the disease in question — defined on the basis of demographic or environmental factors.

- Cervical cancer: population at risk = females aged 30–70 years.
- Hepatitis B: population at risk = seronegative individuals (those without pre-existing antibodies).

Including immune or non-susceptible individuals in your denominator would underestimate the true burden of disease.

4.2 Prevalence: A Snapshot in Time

The Iceberg Phenomenon of Disease

```
         ____________________________________________

                          /\\
                         / \\
            / DIAGNOSED \\        ◄ Visible above waterline
                    / (symptomatic)\\
 -------______________________------- WATERLINE (clinical threshold)
                   /             \\
        / SUBCLINICAL CASES  \\  ◄ Hidden below waterline
                / (asymptomatic,       \\
               /  undiagnosed,         \\
              /   mild infections)      \\
            /_____________________________\\

         ____________________________________________
```

Prevalence surveys reveal the WHOLE iceberg (diagnosed + undiagnosed).
Routine surveillance captures primarily the visible tip.
Implication: true disease burden is ALWAYS higher than reported cases.

Prevalence is the proportion of a defined population that has a disease at a given point in time (or over a period of time). Think of prevalence as a photograph — it captures everyone who has the disease right now, whether they got it yesterday or ten years ago.

Formula: Prevalence (P) = (Number of people with disease at time t) / (Population at risk at time t) x 10n

Table 4.1: Factors That Increase or Decrease Prevalence

Type	Definition	Example
Point Prevalence	Disease frequency at a SINGLE point in time — a snapshot	15 out of 150 school children need glasses = 10% point prevalence
Period Prevalence	Disease frequency over a defined PERIOD of time (existing cases + new cases during the period)	25 existing + 15 new cases in 150 persons = 40/150 = 27% period prevalence

Factors That Influence Prevalence

Table 4.2: Factors That Influence Prevalence (Continued)

Prevalence INCREASES When...	Prevalence DECREASES When...
Illness lasts a long time (long duration)	Illness resolves quickly — rapid cure or rapid death (short duration)
Cure rate is low	Cure rate is high
Case fatality is low	Case fatality is high
Incidence is high (many new cases entering)	Incidence is low (few new cases)

Diseased people migrate INTO the population	Diseased people migrate OUT of the population
Better detection methods find more existing cases	Healthy people migrate IN (dilutes the pool of cases)
Emigration of healthy people from the population	Improved treatment programmes shortening disease duration

Uses of Prevalence Data

- Assess healthcare needs and plan health services at local, national, or global level.
- Measure the burden of disease in a population.
- Measure occurrence of conditions with gradual onset (e.g., chronic diseases).
- Especially useful for chronic diseases where incidence is difficult to measure.

4.3 Incidence: Measuring the Pace of New Disease

Incidence measures new cases only — how fast the disease is appearing in a previously disease-free population. If prevalence is a photograph, incidence is a video recording the rate at which new people enter the 'sick' category.

Table 4.3: Types of Incidence Measures

Measure	Also Called	Formula	Key Feature
Cumulative Incidence (CI)	Attack Rate or Risk	CI = New cases / Population at risk at start x 10n	Assumes the entire at-risk population was followed for the full observation period
Incidence Rate / Incidence Density (ID)	Incidence Rate	ID = New cases / Total Person-Time observed x 10n	Accounts for variable follow-up time; more precise when people drop out or join at different times

Person-Time explained: If one person is followed for 10 years, they contribute 10 person-years. If 10 people are each followed for 1 year, they also contribute 10 person-years. Person-time accounts for the reality that people enter and leave studies at different times.

Risk: The probability that an individual will experience a health status change over a specified follow-up period, assuming they do not have the disease at the start and do not die from other causes during follow-up. Corresponds to cumulative incidence.

Uses of Incidence Data

- Describes trends in diseases over time.

- Evaluates the impact of primary prevention programmes.

4.4 The Prevalence–Incidence Relationship: P = I × D

One of the most elegant formulas in epidemiology relates three key measures:

Prevalence = Incidence × Duration

Conceptual Diagram: The P = I × D Relationship

PREVALENCE (P) = INCIDENCE (I) × DURATION (D)

▼ ▼ ▼

All existing cases (old+new) | New cases per unit time | How long disease lasts on average

HIGH Duration → HIGH Prevalence (e.g., Diabetes)
LOW Duration → LOW Prevalence (e.g., Common cold)
HIGH Incidence → HIGH Prevalence (e.g., TB in endemic area)

Exam tip: P = I × D is the single most tested formula in epidemiology.

Table 4.4: The P = I × D Relationship

Pattern	Example Disease	Explanation
High Prevalence + Low Incidence	Diabetes mellitus	Chronic disease — cases accumulate over many years even if the annual rate of new cases is modest
Low Prevalence + High Incidence	Common cold	Short duration — cases resolve quickly despite a very high rate of new cases appearing constantly

4.5 Case Fatality: How Deadly Is It?

Case Fatality = (Number of deaths from a disease) / (Number of cases of that disease)

Case fatality reflects the severity of a disease — once you have it, what is the chance of dying from it? Note: despite commonly being called the ‘Case Fatality Rate’, it is technically a proportion, not a rate. Importantly, high case fatality also decreases prevalence — because the disease kills patients quickly, removing them from the ‘currently diseased’ pool.

4.6 Summary: All Measures at a Glance

Table 4.5: Summary of Disease Frequency Measures

Measure	Type	Time Frame	Denominator	Primary Use
Prevalence	Static	Point or Period	Population at risk	Burden; chronic disease planning; health service needs
Cumulative Incidence	Dynamic	Over a period	Population at risk at start	Risk estimation; prevention programme evaluation
Incidence Rate (Incidence Density)	Dynamic	Over a period	Person-time of observation	Precise rate when follow-up is variable
Mortality Rate	Rate	Over a period	Total population	Burden of death in the population
Case Fatality	Proportion	Any	Number of cases	Severity of disease; prognosis

Key Takeaways — Chapter 4

- Prevalence = existing cases (old + new). Incidence = NEW cases only.
- P = I × D is exam gold. Memorise it.
- Long duration disease = HIGH prevalence (diabetes). Short duration = LOW prevalence (common cold).
- Case fatality = severity of disease (a proportion, not truly a rate).
- Incidence Rate (Incidence Density) uses person-time as the denominator — vital when follow-up varies.
- Point prevalence = snapshot; Period prevalence = over a time window.

Chapter 5: Watching Without Interfering — Descriptive Study Designs: The Art of Careful Observation Before Jumping to Conclusions

In 1981, five gay men in Los Angeles were diagnosed with Pneumocystis carinii pneumonia — a lung infection usually only seen in severely immunocompromised patients. This was written up as a case series: five patients, an unusual disease, no explanation. That case series triggered one of the most consequential investigations in the history of medicine: the discovery of AIDS. Not bad for a descriptive study.

5.1 The Landscape of Epidemiological Study Designs

Table 5.1: Landscape of Epidemiological Study Designs

Category	Sub-Type	Examples
Descriptive — Individual Level	Case Report / Case Series	A single unusual patient; a group of patients with the same rare disease
Descriptive — Population Level	Ecological Studies	Comparing disease rates across countries or regions using aggregate data
Descriptive / Analytical — Individual	Cross-Sectional Survey	National health surveys; census; NFHS

Analytical — Observational	Cohort; Case-Control; Analytical Cross-Sectional	Framingham Heart Study; Doll and Hill smoking study
Analytical — Experimental	Randomised Controlled Trials (RCTs)	Drug trials; vaccine trials

5.2 Case Reports: One Patient, One Story

A case report is a detailed account of a single patient with unusual or new clinical manifestations — rare disease presentations, unexpected drug reactions, or peculiar imaging findings that have not been previously described.

- **Purpose:** Educate other clinicians; share experience; generate hypotheses about pathophysiological mechanisms.
- **Who benefits:** Fellow clinicians who may encounter a similar presentation and have no idea what they are looking at.
- **Limitation:** No comparison group. You cannot establish causality from one patient. You cannot generalise to any population.
- **Where published:** Usually in dedicated sections of peer-reviewed journals.

5.3 Case Series: More Data, Same Fundamental Limitation

A case series is a study of a relatively larger group of patients — typically ten or more — with the same disease or unusual clinical condition. It is essentially several case reports presented together.

- **Purpose:** Determine whether observed clinical findings are due to the disease itself or merely chance; characterise the clinical picture of a newly recognised disease.
- **Historical example:** Five gay men with PCP in 1981 — the case series that triggered the discovery of AIDS.
- **Limitation:** Still no comparison group. You know what is happening in your patients, but you have nothing to compare them against.

Exam Insight

- Case report = 1 patient. Case series = multiple patients (typically 10 or more).
- NEITHER has a comparison group. Therefore, NEITHER can establish causality.
- The 5 PCP cases in 1981 leading to AIDS discovery is a favourite exam fact.

5.4 Ecological Studies: The View from Above

In ecological studies, the unit of analysis is not the individual — it is a group, region, or population. You might compare per capita fat consumption across 20 different countries with the coronary artery disease rate in each country. If fat-rich countries have more heart disease, that is an ecological association.

- **What is measured:** Aggregate or group-level exposures and outcomes — individual-level data is NOT available.
- **Purpose:** Generate hypotheses about population-level associations; useful when individual-level data is unavailable.
- **Major limitation:** The Ecological Fallacy — the assumption that a group-level association applies to the individuals within that group.

Classic illustration: Countries with high chocolate consumption also have high numbers of Nobel Prize winners. Would you conclude that eating chocolate makes people smarter? That is ecological fallacy in action — delicious but wrong.

Important: The Ecological Fallacy

- Ecological studies use GROUP data, not individual data.
- Group-level associations CANNOT be assumed to apply to individuals within that group.
- This is called the ecological fallacy — the defining limitation of this design.

5.5 Cross-Sectional Studies: The Population Snapshot

Cross-sectional studies observe a defined population at a single point in time. They measure exposures and outcomes simultaneously — like a photograph of the population's health status on a given day. The national census, conducted every ten years, is the classic example. Cross-sectional studies are the most commonly used study design in epidemiology.

Uses of Cross-Sectional Surveys

- Measure the burden and prevalence of disease — how many people in India have hypertension?
- Measure the burden of risk behaviours — e.g., alcohol consumption patterns.
- Understand the distribution of health problems by time, place, and person.
- Provide data for planning health services at state, national, or global level.
- Set priorities for disease control programmes.
- Generate hypotheses about risk factors (when used as an analytical cross-sectional study).
- Evaluate intervention effectiveness using before vs. after comparisons.
- Examples: NFHS (National Family Health Survey), exit surveys, school surveys.

Advantages	Limitations
Quick to plan and complete	Cannot establish temporality — which came first, exposure or disease?
Less expensive than cohort studies	Not suitable for rare diseases
Can measure multiple exposures and outcomes simultaneously	Measures PREVALENCE, not incidence
Suitable for large and diverse populations	Susceptible to the chicken-and-egg problem
Can be done in any setting: school, clinic, community	Selection bias from prevalent (surviving) cases

Table 5.2: Advantages and Limitations of Cross-Sectional Studies

Common Confusion: The Chicken-and-Egg Problem In a cross-sectional study, exposure and outcome are measured at the same time. So if sedentary people have more heart disease, you cannot tell: did inactivity cause the heart disease, or did heart disease make people inactive? This is the TEMPORALITY problem — and it is the defining limitation of cross-sectional designs.

5.6 Comparing All Descriptive Designs

Table 5.3: Comparison of Descriptive Study Designs

Design	Unit of Study	Comparison Group?	Main Use	Key Limitation
Case Report	Single patient	No	Document rare/new manifestations; hypothesis generation	No generalisability
Case Series	Multiple patients (10+)	No	Characterise disease picture; test chance vs. true disease	No comparison group
Ecological	Population or group	Groups compared	Generate population-level hypotheses; use existing data	Ecological fallacy; no individual data
Cross-Sectional	Individual	Can have one (analytical)	Measure disease/risk factor prevalence; plan services	Cannot establish temporality

Key Takeaways — Chapter 5

- Case report = 1 patient; Case series = multiple patients (10+); neither has a comparison group.
- Ecological study: GROUP is the unit of analysis. Ecological fallacy is the major limitation.
- Cross-sectional = snapshot; measures PREVALENCE, not incidence.
- Cross-sectional CANNOT establish temporality — the chicken-and-egg problem.
- Census = cross-sectional survey of the entire population.
- Cross-sectional is the MOST COMMONLY USED study design in epidemiology.

Chapter 6: Finding Causes — Analytical Study Designs: From Careful Observation to Testing Whether X Actually Causes Y

The word 'cohort' comes from the Roman army — a cohort was a unit of 300 to 600 soldiers who marched forward together. In epidemiology, a cohort study does exactly the same thing: it takes a group of people and follows them forward in time to see who develops disease. The key word is 'forward'. Cohort studies move from exposure to outcome, from cause to effect.

Analytical studies help distinguish association from causation.

6.1 What Makes a Study Analytical?

An analytical study has a comparison group. The investigator does NOT assign exposures — they carefully observe and measure who has been exposed and who has not, then compare the rates of disease between the two groups. The goal is to draw inferences about the relationship between exposure and disease.

6.2 Cohort Studies: Following People Forward

A cohort study selects exposed and unexposed groups and follows them forward in time to compare the incidence of disease. Direction: Exposure → Outcome.

Table 6.1: Types of Cohort Studies (Prospective vs. Retrospective)

Type	When Exposure Occurred	When Outcome Assessed	Classic Example
Prospective Cohort	Has NOT yet occurred at study start	Will occur in the future	Framingham Heart Study (1940s): followed ~28,000 residents to identify cardiovascular risk factors
Retrospective Cohort	Has ALREADY occurred at study start	Has ALREADY occurred	Aniline dye workers: 4,622 workers recruited from historical records (1920–1951); bladder cancer deaths reviewed
Bidirectional (Ambispective)	Has ALREADY occurred at study start	Will occur in the future	Exposure already happened but follow-up continues prospectively

The Four Key Components of a Cohort Study

Table 6.2: Key Components of a Cohort Study

Component	Key Details
1. Selection of study population	From the general population (e.g., Framingham) OR special exposure groups (e.g., occupational workers, nurses' cohorts)
2. Baseline assessment	Assess exposure status; collect demographic details; EXCLUDE anyone already with the disease at enrolment; collect data on all known confounders
3. Comparison group	INTERNAL: unexposed subjects from the same population (e.g., normotensive people in Framingham) | EXTERNAL: general population statistics when all study subjects are exposed (e.g., aniline dye study used national cancer mortality rates)
4. Follow-up	Uniform surveillance in BOTH groups; standardised diagnosis throughout — especially important for long studies; complete exposure and outcome ascertainment. Loss to follow-up is the Achilles' heel.

Calculating Relative Risk (RR)

The measure of association in a cohort study is the Relative Risk (RR) — also called the Risk Ratio. Here is how to calculate it from a standard 2x2 table:

Table 6.3: 2×2 Contingency Table for Cohort Studies

	Disease (+)	Disease (-)	Total
Exposed (+)	a	b	a+b
Unexposed (-)	c	d	c+d
Total	a+c	b+d	a+b+c+d

Incidence in exposed = a / (a+b) | Incidence in unexposed = c / (c+d)

Relative Risk (RR) = [a/(a+b)] / [c/(c+d)]

RR Value	Meaning	Interpretation
RR = 1	Incidence identical in both groups	Exposure is NOT associated with disease
RR > 1	Higher incidence in the exposed group	Exposure is POSITIVELY associated — a risk factor
RR < 1	Lower incidence in the exposed group	Exposure is NEGATIVELY associated — a protective factor

Strengths and Weaknesses of Cohort Studies

Table 6.4: Strengths and Weaknesses of Cohort Studies

Strengths	Weaknesses
Can directly calculate incidence and risk	Requires a large sample size
Can examine multiple outcomes for a given exposure	Time-consuming and expensive
Provides strong evidence for temporality — exposure precedes outcome	Not suitable for rare diseases or diseases with very long latency
Especially useful for studying RARE EXPOSURES	Loss to follow-up can introduce serious bias

6.3 Case-Control Studies: Working Backwards

If cohort studies go forward from exposure to outcome, case-control studies work in reverse. You start with people who already have the disease (cases) and people who do not (controls), and then look backwards to compare how often each group was exposed to the suspected risk factor. Classic example: Doll and Hill's landmark study in the 1950s demonstrating the link between cigarette smoking and lung cancer.

The Four Key Components of a Case-Control Study

Table 6.5: Key Components of a Case-Control Study

Component	Key Points
1. Selection of Cases	Clear definition of who counts as a 'case'. Selection must be INDEPENDENT of exposure status. Prefer INCIDENT cases (newly diagnosed) over prevalent cases — prevalent cases reflect survival bias, not just disease development. Sources: hospitals/clinics (convenient but may over-represent severe cases) OR population-based registries (more representative, e.g., cancer registry)

2. Selection of Controls	Controls represent the distribution of exposure in the SOURCE POPULATION — they are who would have been selected as cases had they developed the disease. Selection must be INDEPENDENT of exposure status. Sources: (a) population-based sample (b) hospital-based patients — used by Doll & Hill (c) friends, neighbours, or family members of cases
3. Data Collection on Exposures	Collect data objectively, accurately, and precisely. Measurements must be reproducible. The major hazard: RECALL BIAS — cases (knowing they are sick) may remember past exposures more intensely or differently than controls
4. Analysis	Calculate the ODDS RATIO (OR) as the measure of association. You CANNOT calculate incidence rates because you selected fixed numbers of cases and controls at the outset.

Calculating the Odds Ratio (OR)

Table 6.6: 2×2 Contingency Table for Case-Control Studies

	Cases (Disease +)	Controls (Disease -)	Total
Exposed (+)	a	b	a+b
Unexposed (-)	c	d	c+d
Total	a+c	b+d	a+b+c+d

Odds of exposure among cases = a / c

Odds of exposure among controls = b / d

Odds Ratio (OR) = (a/c) / (b/d) = ad / bc (The Cross-Product Ratio)

OR Value	Meaning	Interpretation
OR = 1	Odds of exposure equal in cases and controls	Exposure is NOT associated with disease
OR > 1	Higher odds of exposure among cases	Exposure is POSITIVELY associated — a risk factor
OR < 1	Lower odds of exposure among cases	Exposure is NEGATIVELY associated — a protective factor

Strengths and Weaknesses of Case-Control Studies

Table 6.7: Strengths and Weaknesses of Case-Control Studies

Strengths	Weaknesses
Ideal for RARE diseases or long-latency diseases	Susceptible to recall bias

Quick and relatively inexpensive to conduct	Appropriate control selection is difficult
Requires fewer subjects than cohort studies	Cannot calculate incidence or risk
Can examine MULTIPLE exposures simultaneously	Cannot definitively establish temporality

6.4 Head-to-Head: Cohort vs. Case-Control

Study Flow: Cohort Study vs. Case-Control Study

COHORT STUDY	CASE-CONTROL STUDY
Start with EXPOSURE	Start with OUTCOME
▼	▼
Exposed group Unexposed group	Cases (with disease) Controls (without disease)
▼	▼
Follow forward in time	Look backwards in time
▼	▼
Measure: Incidence	Measure: Past exposure
▼	▼
Calculate: Relative Risk (RR)	Calculate: Odds Ratio (OR)
Direction: Exposure → Outcome Time: Prospective (usually) Best for: Common outcomes	Direction: Outcome → Exposure Time: Retrospective (usually) Best for: Rare outcomes

Table 6.8: Cohort vs. Case-Control: Head-to-Head Comparison

Feature	Cohort Study	Case-Control Study
Direction	Exposure → Outcome (forward)	Outcome → Exposure (backward)
Starting point	Exposed vs. unexposed individuals	Cases vs. controls
Measure of association	Relative Risk (RR)	Odds Ratio (OR)
Can calculate incidence?	YES — directly measured	NO — fixed numbers selected at the start
Best for studying...	RARE EXPOSURES	RARE DISEASES or long-latency diseases
Time and cost	Long duration; expensive	Quick; relatively inexpensive
Main bias concern	Loss to follow-up bias	Recall bias
Classic example	Framingham Heart Study (CV risk factors)	Doll and Hill (smoking and lung cancer)

Key Takeaways — Chapter 6

- Cohort: Exposure → Outcome; measures Relative Risk (RR); best for rare exposures.
- Case-control: Outcome → Exposure; measures Odds Ratio (OR); best for rare diseases.
- OR = ad/bc (cross-product ratio). RR = [a/(a+b)] / [c/(c+d)].
- Cohort CAN calculate incidence; case-control CANNOT.
- Framingham = classic prospective cohort; Doll & Hill = classic case-control.
- Recall bias = major weakness of case-control studies.
- Prefer INCIDENT cases in case-control — prevalent cases reflect survival, not disease onset.

Chapter 7: The Gold Standard — Experimental Designs and Clinical Trials: When Observing Is Not Enough and You Have to Take Charge

Consider how the drugs in your pharmacy cabinet reached the shelf. Someone had an idea. Someone tested it in a lab. Then, eventually, someone designed a rigorous trial in human beings, compared it fairly against the best existing treatment, and demonstrated that it actually works. That process — the clinical trial — is the gold standard of scientific evidence. Without it, medicine would be guesswork dressed in a white coat.

7.1 Definition and Purpose of Clinical Trials

A clinical trial is a planned, prospective experiment designed to assess the efficacy or safety of prophylactic, diagnostic, or therapeutic agents, devices, procedures, or regimens in human subjects. Outcomes in two or more groups are compared after assigning participants to different interventions.

The key word distinguishing clinical trials from all observational studies: the INVESTIGATOR MANIPULATES the exposure. This is what makes them experimental.

Clinical trials are used to evaluate:

- New drugs and pharmaceutical agents.
- New treatments and medical technologies.
- New methods of primary prevention — vaccines being the most important example.

- New screening programmes for early disease detection.
- New healthcare delivery or organisational systems.

7.2 Classification of Study Designs

Table 7.1: Classification of Study Designs

Category	Sub-type	Example	Nature
Observational	Descriptive	Cross-sectional, Ecological, Case series	No manipulation of exposure
Observational	Analytical (retrospective)	Case-control study	No manipulation
Observational	Analytical (prospective)	Cohort study	No manipulation
Experimental	Planned	Clinical Trial (RCT)	Investigator MANIPULATES exposure

7.3 The Four Phases of Clinical Trials

Drug development follows a sequential, phased approach. Each phase builds on the previous one with progressively larger and sicker populations.

Table 7.2: The Four Phases of Clinical Trials

Phase	Sample Size	Participants	Primary Goal
Phase I	< 50	Healthy volunteers	Safety and acceptability — can humans even tolerate this?
Phase II	100 – 500	Low-risk or mildly affected patients	Long-term safety, dose and schedule optimisation, early efficacy signals
Phase III	Thousands	High-risk or diseased patients	Efficacy under controlled conditions — the basis for regulatory approval and drug licensing
Phase IV	Thousands+	General community (post-marketing)	Post-marketing surveillance; detection of rare adverse events not seen in smaller trials

7.4 Randomisation: The Great Equaliser

Randomisation is the process ensuring that every participant has an equal chance of being assigned to any arm of the trial. Neither the participant nor the investigator decides the assignment — it is done through a neutral, third-party process.

Why randomise? Because it:

- Makes the groups as similar as possible at baseline — so any differences in outcomes are due to the intervention, not pre-existing differences.
- Controls for BOTH known AND unknown confounders automatically — something no statistical adjustment can do.
- Minimises selection bias in group assignment.
- Reduces co-intervention bias.

7.5 Blinding: What You Don't Know Can't Bias You

Even after randomisation, if participants know which group they are in, they may behave differently (the placebo effect). If investigators know which participants received the active treatment, they may unconsciously assess outcomes differently. Blinding prevents both.

Table 7.3: Types of Blinding in Clinical Trials

Type	Who Is Blinded	What It Prevents
Single-blind	Participant only	Placebo effect and exaggeration of subjective symptoms by the participant
Double-blind	Participant + Investigator	Researcher bias in data collection and outcome ascertainment
Triple-blind	Participant + Investigator + Data Analyst	All subjective biases throughout the trial; the most rigorous form

Co-intervention bias: occurs when participants who know their treatment group seek out or exchange additional interventions on their own. Blinding prevents this.

7.6 Therapeutic vs. Prevention Trials

Table 7.4: Therapeutic vs. Prevention Trials

Feature	Therapeutic Trial	Prevention Trial
Study population	Persons who ALREADY have the disease	Susceptible or at-risk persons WITHOUT the disease
Comparator arm	Standard treatment (e.g., existing drug regimen)	Placebo OR existing vaccine
Primary outcome	Cure rate or clinical improvement	Disease incidence in each arm
Example	New HIV drug regimen vs. standard HAART	New vaccine vs. placebo in an uninfected high-risk population

7.7 Advantages and Limitations of Clinical Trials

Table 7.5: Advantages and Limitations of Clinical Trials

Advantages	Limitations
The primary design that effectively controls selection bias through randomisation	Complex; requires extensive training and infrastructure
Controls confounding without statistical adjustment	Expensive to design and execute
Facilitates effective blinding	Limited generalisability — the trial sample may not represent the real-world population
Maintains the benefits of a prospective design	Significant ethical challenges, especially when withholding a potential benefit

Key Takeaways — Chapter 7

- Clinical trials = the gold standard. Investigator MANIPULATES the exposure.
- Phase I: safety, <50 healthy volunteers. Phase II: dose+safety, 100–500. Phase III: efficacy, thousands (basis for licensing). Phase IV: post-marketing surveillance.
- Randomisation gives every participant an EQUAL CHANCE of assignment — controls known AND unknown confounders.
- Single-blind = patient blinded. Double-blind = patient + investigator. Triple-blind = all three.
- Therapeutic trials: diseased patients. Prevention trials: at-risk individuals.

Chapter 8: Can You Trust Your Results? — Validity, Bias, and Confounding: The Three Gremlins That Live Inside Every Study

You have run your study, collected your data, and found that coffee drinkers have twice the risk of heart attack. Before you ban espresso nationally, ask yourself: could this be chance? A flaw in how you selected participants? A measurement error? Or is smoking — which is more common among coffee drinkers — actually the real culprit? These are the questions of validity, and they are the most important questions in all of epidemiology.

Trust is rarely double-blind.

8.1 Internal and External Validity

Table 8.1: Internal vs. External Validity

Type	Definition	Threatened By
Internal Validity	Accuracy of the estimated association WITHIN the study — does the result truly reflect what happened in your study sample?	Selection bias, information bias, confounding
External Validity (Generalisability)	The ability to apply the study's findings to the broader target population beyond the study sample	Non-representative samples; highly restricted eligibility criteria

Critical Rule: A study WITHOUT internal validity CANNOT have external validity. Internal validity is a PREREQUISITE for generalisability. You must get the inside right before projecting outward.

8.2 Types of Error

Table 8.2: Types of Error in Research

Error Type	Cause	Effect	How to Reduce
Random Error (Chance)	Uncontrollable variability; sampling error; measurement imprecision	Reduces precision; does NOT cause systematic distortion in one direction	Larger sample size; repeated measurements
Systematic Error (Bias)	Flaws in study design, data collection, or analysis	Threatens validity; can distort results consistently in one direction	Careful design; blinding; standardised protocols

SIC — The Three Threats to Validity

- S = Selection Bias | I = Information Bias | C = Confounding
- If your study is SIC, your results are untrustworthy.

8.3 Selection Bias: Garbage In, Garbage Out

Selection bias occurs when the procedures used to select study participants result in a sample that does not accurately represent the target population — creating a systematic difference between those selected and those not selected.

Table 8.3: Types of Selection Bias

Study Type	Common Mechanism	Example
Case-Control	Survival bias — only living cases are enrolled	Dead cases (who may have had different exposures) are missed entirely
Case-Control	Hospital-based design	Cases and controls from one hospital may share hospital-related exposures unrelated to the study question
Case-Control	Differential surveillance or diagnosis	Exposed group diagnosed more vigorously than unexposed group
Cohort	Loss to follow-up	More-exposed or higher-risk persons more likely to drop out, distorting outcome rates

Prevention Strategies for Selection Bias

- Use INCIDENT (newly diagnosed) rather than prevalent cases.
- Use population-based (community) designs instead of hospital-based designs.
- Apply identical eligibility criteria to cases and controls.
- Use the same diagnostic procedures and surveillance intensity for both groups.
- Minimise non-response and loss to follow-up; record baseline data on dropouts.
- Apply blinding at the disease diagnosis stage.

Detection at Analysis Stage

- Compare dropouts vs. retained participants on baseline characteristics.
- Perform sensitivity analysis to test the direction and magnitude of potential bias.

8.4 Information Bias: The Measurement Problem

Information bias — also called measurement bias — arises from errors in measuring exposure, outcome, or confounding variables. The result is misclassification: people end up in the wrong category.

Table 8.4: Types of Information Bias

Study Type	Mechanism	Named Bias
Case-Control	Diseased people recall past exposures more intensely or differently than healthy controls	Recall Bias
Case-Control	Better exposure data available for cases than for controls	Differential Misclassification
Cohort	Exposed group followed and examined more rigorously than unexposed group	Surveillance / Detection Bias
All types	Investigator systematically collects information differently across groups	Observer / Interviewer Bias
All types	Participants deliberately distort what they report	Reporting Bias

Prevention Strategies for Information Bias

- Set precise operational definitions for all variables before the study begins.
- Develop and follow detailed measurement protocols; use standard instruments.
- Use repeated measurements on key variables (e.g., take the average of three blood pressure readings).
- Ensure all investigators are trained, certified, and supervised.

- Conduct regular data audits throughout the study.
- Clean data before analysis and re-run analysis before publication.

8.5 Confounding: The Third-Wheel Problem

Confounding comes from the French for 'confusion of effects'. A confounder is a third variable associated with BOTH the exposure AND the outcome — and is NOT on the causal pathway between them. It is what makes coffee appear to cause lung cancer when smoking is the real culprit.

Confounding can harm your study in four distinct ways:

- Simulate a false association — show one where none exists.
- Hide a true association — mask an existing one.
- Exaggerate or attenuate the true strength of association.
- Reverse the direction of effect — the most dangerous scenario of all.

Control of Confounding

Table 8.5: Methods to Control Confounding

Stage	Method	How It Works
Design	Restriction	Limit participants to one stratum of the confounder (e.g., non-smokers only)
Design	Matching	Match cases and controls on known confounders; requires matched analysis
Design	Randomisation	The BEST method — automatically distributes all confounders equally across trial arms
Analysis	Stratified Analysis	Examine the exposure-outcome association within strata of the confounder
Analysis	Multivariate Regression	Simultaneously adjust for multiple confounders using logistic or linear regression

8.6 Evaluating a Crude Association: The 5-Step Spiral

When you find an association in your data, do not immediately declare victory. Work through these five questions before concluding that the association is causal:

Table 8.6: The 5-Step Spiral for Evaluating an Association

Step	Question to Ask
1. Chance	Could the association be due to random error? Check the p-value and confidence intervals.
2. Selection Bias	Could the way participants were selected explain the association?
3. Information Bias	Could measurement errors — recall bias, observer bias — explain or distort the association?
4. Confounding	Could a third variable explain or distort the observed association?
5. Causation?	Only after ruling out all of the above can you consider the association potentially causal.

Classic Exam Case: Coffee and Heart Attack

- Association seen: Coffee drinkers appear to have a higher risk of myocardial infarction.
- Selection bias: Hospital patients (with gastric ulcers caused by coffee) over-represent coffee drinkers among controls.
- Information bias: Inaccurate recall of coffee quantities; some chest pain misclassified as MI.
- Confounding: Smoking is associated with both coffee drinking AND MI — the coffee-MI link may be entirely due to smoking.
- Conclusion: Apply the 5-step spiral before calling ANYTHING causal. Coffee is probably innocent.

Key Takeaways — Chapter 8

- Internal validity = accuracy within the study. It is a PREREQUISITE for external validity.
- Three threats: Selection bias (S), Information bias (I), Confounding (C) — SIC.
- Random error → larger sample size. Bias → better study design.
- Recall bias is the major weakness of case-control studies.
- Confounding can simulate, hide, exaggerate, or REVERSE associations.
- Before concluding causation: rule out chance → selection bias → information bias → confounding.

Chapter 9: Numbers and Words — Quantitative and Qualitative Research: Statistics Without the Terror, and Asking 'Why' Without a Questionnaire

Quantitative research tells you HOW MANY people are doing something. Qualitative research tells you WHY they are doing it. Both matter. You need the numbers to know the scale of a problem. You need the words to understand what is really going on beneath the surface.

When reality disagrees, statistics still agrees.

Part A: Quantitative Measurement

9.1 Classification of Data

Before you can analyse data, you need to know what type you have. Different data types require fundamentally different statistical approaches. Getting this wrong at the start means your entire analysis is built on the wrong foundation.

Table 9.1: Classification of Data Types

Category	Sub-Type	Definition	Example
Qualitative (Categorical)	Nominal	Categories with NO natural order or ranking	Eye colour, blood group, religion, region
Qualitative (Categorical)	Ordinal	Categories WITH a natural order or ranking, but the gaps between ranks are not necessarily equal	Disease severity: mild, moderate, severe
Quantitative (Numerical)	Discrete	Countable whole-number values only; cannot take fractional values	Number of siblings; number of hospital admissions
Quantitative (Numerical)	Continuous	Can take any value on a continuous scale, including fractions	Height, weight, blood pressure, age, fasting blood sugar

Exam Tip: Data Types and Appropriate Statistics

- Nominal data: Mode is the most appropriate measure — no mathematical ordering exists.
- Ordinal data: use MEDIAN and mode — you can rank but not meaningfully add.
- Continuous data: use MEAN, standard deviation, and parametric tests.
- Different data types need different statistical tests — this is a common exam question.

9.2 Measures of Central Tendency

A measure of central tendency represents the 'typical' or 'central' value in a dataset. There are three: mean, median, and mode — and choosing the wrong one is a common mistake.

Table 9.2: Measures of Central Tendency

Measure	Definition / Formula	When to Use	Key Limitation
Mean (Arithmetic Mean)	Sum of all values divided by n. Sample = x-bar; Population = mu	Continuous data with no extreme outliers; symmetric distribution	Heavily distorted by extreme values (outliers)
Median	Middle value when data is ordered; 50th percentile. Position = (n+1)/2; average of middle two if n is even	Skewed data; data with outliers; ordinal data	Does not use all values in its calculation
Mode	Most frequently occurring value. A dataset can have no mode, one	Nominal data; epidemic curves	May not be unique; not

	mode (unimodal), or multiple modes (bimodal, multimodal)	(modal class = peak of outbreak; used to estimate incubation period)	useful for continuous data in most analyses

Worked example — Mean vs. Median: Hospital stay (days) for 11 patients: 1, 2, 3, 4, 5, 6, 7, 8, 9, 9, 77. Mean = 11.8 days (badly inflated by the outlier '77'). Median = 6 days (6th value, unaffected by the outlier). For this skewed data, the median gives a far more representative picture.

Mode example: Colour preferences — Green: 354, Yellow: 852, White: 310, Red: 474. Mode = Yellow (highest frequency). In epidemic curves, the modal class (the peak interval) is used to estimate the incubation period of the causative agent.

9.3 Measures of Dispersion (Spread)

A central tendency tells you where the middle is. Dispersion tells you how spread out the data is around that middle. Both together give a complete picture of the data.

Table 9.3: Measures of Dispersion

Measure	Definition	Advantage	Disadvantage
Range	Maximum value minus Minimum value	Quick and easy to calculate	Affected by extreme values; uses only 2 data points
Inter-Quartile Range (IQR = Q3 - Q1)	Spread of the middle 50% of data; removes the top and bottom 25% before calculating	NOT affected by extreme values; robust to outliers	Uses only the middle 50%; still uses only 2 values
Mean Deviation from Mean	Average of absolute differences from the mean (signs ignored to avoid sum = 0)	Uses all observations; conceptually simple	Ignores sign of differences; mathematically less rigorous
Variance	Average of squared deviations from the mean; squaring removes negative signs	Uses all observations; mathematically rigorous	Units are SQUARED — not in same units as original data
Standard Deviation (SD)	Square root of variance; same units as the original data	Most important measure of spread; used in further statistical tests	Sensitive to extreme values (outliers)
Coefficient of Variation (CV)	(SD / Mean) x 100% — a dimensionless percentage	Allows comparison of variability across groups with different units or scales	Meaningless if mean is zero or near-zero

9.4 Choosing the Right Summary Statistics

Table 9.4: Choosing the Right Summary Statistics

Data Type	Central Tendency	Dispersion	Notes
Continuous (symmetric, no outliers)	Mean	Standard Deviation	Most powerful; used in further parametric statistical tests
Continuous (skewed or with outliers)	Median	IQR	Robust; can use log-transformation then mean if needed
Ordinal	Median	IQR or Range	Mode may also be reported
Nominal	Mode	Range (counts)	Frequency tables are the standard presentation
Epidemic curve (time distribution)	Mode (modal class)	Range	Modal class helps estimate incubation period

Part B: Qualitative Research Methods

9.5 What Is Qualitative Research?

Qualitative research explores the 'why' and 'how' behind health behaviours, beliefs, and decisions. It produces text-based rather than numerical data, and takes an interpretive, inductive approach rooted in the traditions of anthropology, sociology, and psychology. Where quantitative research counts, qualitative research explains.

Table 9.5: Quantitative vs. Qualitative Research

Feature	Quantitative	Qualitative
Data type	Numbers and measurements	Words, text, and narratives
Perspective	Objective (investigator's view imposed on the world)	Subjective / emic (participant's own perspective)
Logic of inquiry	Deductive — tests pre-specified hypotheses	Inductive — generates theories from the data
Research design	Fixed, structured, and reproducible	Emergent, flexible, and iterative
Validity	Statistical validity	Credibility of responses and investigator interpretation
Generalisation	Statistical generalisation across populations	Conceptual / abstract; transcends cultures rather than populations

9.6 When to Use Qualitative Methods

- To understand WHY and HOW health events or behaviours occur.
- When the subject matter is insufficiently researched or the vocabulary is unfamiliar.

- To obtain insight into meanings, attitudes, beliefs, and perceptions.
- To view a social phenomenon holistically from the participants' own perspective.
- To understand the determinants of health behaviour and why interventions succeed or fail.
- As a preliminary step to generate items for a quantitative questionnaire.

9.7 The Three Main Qualitative Methods

A. In-Depth Interviews (IDIs)

One-to-one, open-ended interviews following a flexible interview guide. The investigator uses probes to obtain richer, contextualised information. Data is recorded verbatim.

When to Use IDIs	Advantages	Disadvantages
Complex, sensitive subject matter (sexual behaviour, drug use)	Most in-depth understanding of individual behaviour and experience	Not generalisable — small, purposive sample
Geographically dispersed respondents	Exact language and vocabulary of the participant is captured	Time-consuming to conduct and to analyse
When participant is more knowledgeable than investigator about the topic	Insider's perspective (emic view) is obtained	Interpretation depends on the researcher — potential for bias

B. Focus Group Discussions (FGDs)

Open-ended group discussion with 6–8 homogeneous participants. A moderator guides discussion using a flexible guide; a note-taker records proceedings. Audio/video recording is strongly recommended.

When to Use FGDs	Advantages	Disadvantages
When group interaction will generate richer data than individual interviews	Natural way to discuss social norms; interactions between participants add depth	Personal or sensitive topics may not emerge in a group setting
When cost and time efficiency are important	Data from many participants quickly and efficiently	Dominant personalities can skew the discussion
For generating ideas, identifying problems, evaluating interventions	Good for understanding locally used terminology	Transcription and analysis is laborious
To understand community or social norms around health behaviours	Rich social data in limited time	Not generalisable to large populations

C. Participant Observation

The researcher becomes an active participant in the social event or group being studied. This method originates from the ethnographic and anthropological tradition and generates very deep, detailed, first-hand data. The challenge is that it is difficult to systematically record data while actively participating. Analytical methods for this approach are still evolving.

9.8 Analysis of Qualitative Data

Table 9.6: Analysis Methods for Qualitative Data

Approach	Process
Grounded Theory (Inductive: Data → Theory)	Themes emerge from the data itself; theory is built bottom-up without a pre-existing framework
Content Analysis (Deductive: Theory → Data)	Start with a theoretical framework; apply it top-down to code and categorise the data

General analysis steps: transcribe interviews into text (translate if needed); code themes and categories from the text; build relationships between themes; use quotes to illustrate key themes — these replace the numerical tables of quantitative analysis.

9.9 Triangulation: Strength in Multiple Perspectives

Triangulation means examining the same question from multiple angles — using different methods, data sources, or analysts — to check for consistency and reduce selective interpretive bias.

Type	Description
Method triangulation	Use both quantitative AND qualitative methods on the same research question
Analyst triangulation	Multiple analysts independently code the same data; findings are compared
Theory triangulation	Apply different theoretical frameworks to interpret the same data
Data-source triangulation	Collect data from different sources; compare and synthesise the differences

9.10 How Qualitative Methods Are Used in Practice

Table 9.7: Applications of Qualitative Methods in Practice

Use	Example
Idea generation (preliminary step)	Develop items for a quantitative questionnaire on open defecation practices

Explaining quantitative findings	Understand WHY a quantitative study found an unexpected result
Primary data collection	In-depth study of why people do or do not use a particular health service
Alongside quantitative (mixed methods)	Concurrent qualitative + quantitative to enrich overall understanding

Key Takeaways — Chapter 9

- Data types: Nominal (no order) → Ordinal (ranked) → Discrete (countable) → Continuous (any value).
- No outliers → Mean + SD. Outliers/skewed → Median + IQR. Nominal → Mode + Range.
- SD = square root of variance; same units as the data; the most important measure of spread.
- Qualitative research = inductive; emic perspective; produces text, not numbers.
- Three qualitative methods: IDI (1:1, sensitive topics), FGD (6–8, social norms), Participant Observation (ethnographic).
- Grounded theory = data → theory (inductive). Content analysis = theory → data (deductive).
- Triangulation uses multiple methods, sources, or analysts to verify and enrich findings.

Chapter 10: Who Gets Into Your Study? — Sampling, Sample Size, and Study Population: The Art and Science of Choosing the Right People

A study is only as good as the people in it. Choose the wrong participants, and your beautifully designed study will produce findings that apply to nobody. Choose too few participants, and you will not have enough statistical power to detect a real effect. Getting the 'who' and the 'how many' right is one of the most critical decisions in the entire research process.

10.1 Why Sample At All?

Imagine you want to know the average blood pressure of every adult in India. Studying all 1.4 billion people is clearly impossible. This is true for almost every research question — the population of interest is simply too large, too spread out, or too expensive to study in its entirety. This is why researchers use sampling.

Sampling means selecting a smaller, representative group of people from the larger population and studying them. If the sample is chosen correctly, the findings from this smaller group can be applied, with confidence, to the entire population.

There are four main reasons why sampling is not just convenient — it is often more accurate than trying to study everyone:

- Time efficiency: Collecting data from millions of people takes years. A well-chosen sample of a few hundred or a few thousand people can give you the same answer in a fraction of the time.
- Greater accuracy: When you study a smaller group, fewer investigators are involved. This reduces inter-observer variation — the tendency for different observers to measure or record things slightly differently — which means your data is actually more reliable.
- Feasibility: Many populations are geographically scattered or difficult to access. Studying a sample is simply more practical.
- Cost: Sampling dramatically reduces the financial and logistical burden of research.

10.2 Key Sampling Terminology

Before discussing how to sample, you need to understand the language used in sampling. These terms appear in exams and research papers constantly.

Table 10.1: Key Sampling Terminology

Term	What It Means (in Plain Language)
Sampling	The process of selecting a smaller group of people from a larger population to represent that population in your study.
Study Population	The specific population to which your results will be applied. This is NOT the same as the general population — it is defined by your research question.
Sampling Unit (BSU)	The individual 'thing' that you are selecting — it could be a person, a hospital, a village, or a health worker, depending on your study.
Sampling Frame	A complete list of every sampling unit in the population. This is the master list from which you actually draw your sample.
Sampling Scheme	The method or technique you use to select units from the sampling frame (e.g., random selection, every 5th person, etc.).
Sampling Error	The difference between the value you measure in your sample and the true value in the whole population. Sampling error is unavoidable but can be minimised.

Exam Tip: Study Population is NOT the General Population

This is a very commonly tested distinction. The study population is always defined by the research question — it is the specific group your study is about, not the entire public.

Example 1: A study on needle-stick injuries among healthcare workers → Study population = All healthcare workers in India.

Example 2: A study on a new hospital immunisation policy → Study population = All hospitals in India (not individual people).

Notice how the same country can have completely different study populations depending on what is being studied.

10.3 Non-Probability vs. Probability Sampling

All sampling methods can be divided into two broad categories: non-probability sampling and probability sampling. Understanding the difference is fundamental, because only one of them allows you to make valid conclusions about the larger population.

Table 10.2: Non-Probability vs. Probability Sampling

Feature	Non-Probability Sampling	Probability Sampling
How selection works	The probability of any person being selected is unknown. The researcher's judgment or convenience drives selection.	Every unit in the population has a known, non-zero probability of being selected. Selection is objective and based on chance.
Risk of bias	High — because the researcher may (consciously or unconsciously) favour certain participants.	Low — because random selection removes the researcher's subjective influence from the process.
Can you use standard statistics?	No — standard statistical tests assume probability sampling. Using them on non-probability samples is technically invalid.	Yes — probability sampling is the foundation on which all standard statistical theory is built.
Can you generalise to the population?	No — you cannot draw valid conclusions about the broader population from a non-probability sample.	Yes — this is the only sampling method that allows valid, defensible generalisation to the population.
When is it used?	Hypothesis generation, exploratory research, pilot studies — situations where you are not yet drawing final conclusions.	Definitive studies, population surveys, any research where you need to make valid population-level inferences.
Examples	Convenience sampling (whoever is available), purposive sampling (researcher hand-picks participants).	Simple random sampling, systematic, stratified, cluster, and multistage sampling.

In summary: non-probability sampling is used when you are exploring or generating ideas. Probability sampling is used when you need answers that actually apply to the real world.

10.4 The Five Types of Probability Sampling

Probability sampling comes in five main forms. Each has a specific logic, specific advantages, and specific situations where it works best.

10.4.1 Simple Random Sampling (SRS)

In simple random sampling, every single individual in the population has an exactly equal chance of being selected. The process works like a lottery: you number every individual in your population, and then use a random number table or a computer to draw the required number of names.

For example, if you have a list of 48 patients and need to select 4, you might use a random number generator and get the numbers 9, 18, 32, and 40. Those four patients become your sample.

Advantage: SRS is conceptually the simplest and most transparent method. Sampling error is easy to calculate, which makes the statistics clean and easy to interpret.

Disadvantage: It requires a complete and accurate list (sampling frame) of every person in the population, which is often difficult or impossible to obtain. There is also a small risk that, by chance, the random selection produces an unusual sample that does not represent the population well.

10.4.2 Systematic Sampling

Systematic sampling is a structured alternative to pure randomness. Instead of randomly selecting every individual, you select every kth unit from an ordered list, where k is called the sampling interval.

The formula is: $k = N \div n$, where N is the total population size and n is the number of people you need to sample.

You start by selecting the first unit randomly from within the first k units, and then select every kth unit after that. For example, if $k = 8$, you randomly pick a starting house (say, house number 3), and then select houses 11, 19, 27, 35, and so on.

Advantage: It is practical and easy to implement in field settings because you do not need to make random selections for each participant — just follow the fixed interval.

Disadvantage: If there is a periodic pattern in your list that coincidentally matches your sampling interval (for example, if every 8th house on a street is always the corner house, which tends to be larger), your sample could be biased without you realising it.

10.4.3 Stratified Sampling

In stratified sampling, you first divide the total population into distinct subgroups called strata. These strata are based on a characteristic that is relevant to your study — for example, gender, age group, geographic region, or socioeconomic status. Then, you independently draw a random sample from each stratum.

For example, if you are studying vaccine coverage across India and you know that coverage varies by region, you might divide India into North, East, South, and West, and then randomly sample from each region separately. This guarantees that all four regions are represented in your final sample.

Advantage: Stratified sampling is more precise than SRS when the variable you are measuring differs between strata. It also allows you to make separate conclusions about each subgroup, which is useful if that is part of your research question.

Disadvantage: Measuring the overall sampling error requires combining estimates across strata, which can be mathematically complex. Also, if a particular stratum has very few people, your estimate for that group will be imprecise.

10.4.4 Cluster Sampling

Cluster sampling works differently from the methods above. Instead of selecting individuals directly, you first randomly select groups (called clusters) — such as villages, schools, or hospitals — and then study all or some individuals within the selected clusters.

The key advantage of this method is that you do NOT need a complete list of every individual in the population before you begin. You only need a list of the clusters. Once a cluster is selected, you create the individual-level list for just that cluster.

A classic example is the WHO Expanded Programme on Immunisation (EPI) vaccination survey, which uses a 30 × 7 cluster design — 30 clusters are randomly selected, and 7 children are sampled within each cluster.

Advantage: No complete population list is needed in advance. Travel and field costs are much lower because data collection is concentrated in specific locations rather than spread across an entire region.

Disadvantage: Cluster sampling has a higher design effect (DEFF > 1) compared to SRS. This is because people within the same cluster tend to be similar to each other (homogeneous), which means each additional person from the same cluster adds less new information than a person selected from somewhere else. This requires you to increase your sample size to compensate.

How Cluster Sampling Works: The Two-Stage PPS Method

In large-scale surveys, cluster sampling is often done using a method called Probability Proportional to Size (PPS), in two stages:

Stage 1 — Selecting clusters (PPS): You create a list of all possible clusters (e.g., all villages) along with their population sizes. You calculate a cumulative population total and a sampling interval (Grand Total ÷ Number of clusters needed). You then choose a random starting number and add the interval repeatedly to identify which clusters are selected. Clusters with larger populations are more likely to be selected because they occupy more space in the cumulative list.

Stage 2 — Selecting individuals within clusters: Once a cluster is selected, you create a complete list of all individuals within that cluster and use simple random sampling to select the required number.

10.4.5 Multistage Sampling

Multistage sampling is the most practical approach for large national surveys. As the name suggests, it involves sampling in multiple stages — for example, first selecting states, then selecting districts within those states, then selecting villages within those districts, then selecting households within those villages, and finally selecting individuals within those households.

This approach is used in major surveys like the National Family Health Survey (NFHS) in India because it is simply not feasible to create a single list of all individuals in a country of 1.4 billion people.

Advantage: No complete population listing is needed at any stage — you only need a list of the units at each stage as you go. This makes it feasible for national-scale research.

Disadvantage: Because sampling errors accumulate at every stage, the overall sampling error is larger and more complex to calculate. The design effect also needs to be accounted for.

Quick Comparison: The Five Probability Sampling Methods

Table 10.3: Comparison of Probability Sampling Methods

Method	Needs Complete List?	Design Effect	Best Used When...
Simple Random Sampling (SRS)	Yes — complete list of all individuals	DEFF = 1 (the standard)	Population is small and a complete list is available.
Systematic Sampling	Yes — ordered list of all individuals	Low (similar to SRS)	You need a simple field method and have an ordered list.
Stratified Sampling	Yes — complete list within each stratum	Low	You need separate estimates for subgroups, or the outcome varies by stratum.
Cluster Sampling	No — only a list of clusters	HIGH (> 1) — must adjust n	No individual list exists; field costs need to be minimised.
Multistage Sampling	No — list built stage by stage	Variable — must adjust n	Large national or regional surveys where no single list exists.

10.5 Calculating Sample Size: There Is No Magic Number

One of the most common questions every researcher asks is: 'How many participants do I need?' The honest answer is: it depends. Sample size must be calculated systematically based on several specific factors. Simply guessing a number — or choosing 100 because it 'sounds reasonable' — is not scientifically acceptable.

A sample that is too small will not have enough statistical power to detect a real effect, meaning your study may conclude 'no difference' even when a difference actually exists. A sample that is unnecessarily large wastes resources, time, and money, and may expose more participants to research risks than necessary.

Core Statistical Concepts You Must Understand

Before you can calculate sample size, you need to understand several key statistical concepts. These are also very frequently tested in examinations.

Table 10.4: Core Statistical Concepts for Sample Size

Concept	Symbol	Typical Value	What It Actually Means
Alpha (Type I Error)	α	0.05 (5%)	The probability of concluding there is an effect when there actually is not one (a false positive). A value of 0.05 means you accept a 5% chance of being wrong in this direction.
Confidence Level	$1 - \alpha$	95%	The probability that your calculated interval actually contains the true population value. A 95% confidence level means if you repeated the study 100 times, your confidence interval would capture the true value 95 times.
Beta (Type II Error)	β	0.20 (20%)	The probability of failing to detect a real effect that actually exists (a false negative). A value of 0.20 means you accept a 20% chance of missing a real difference.
Power	$1 - \beta$	80%	The probability of correctly detecting a real effect when it truly exists. Higher power means your study is better at finding real effects. Power of 80% is the conventional minimum standard.
Precision (d)	d	±5% or ±10%	How close you want your sample estimate to be to the true population value. A smaller d means more precision, but requires a larger sample.
Z-alpha	$z\alpha$	1.96 (for 95% CI)	The value from the standard normal distribution corresponding to your chosen significance level. For $\alpha = 0.05$, this value is 1.96.
Z-beta	$z\beta$	0.84 (for 80% power)	The value from the standard normal distribution corresponding to your chosen power level. For 80% power, this value is 0.84.

Exam Tip: Type I and Type II Errors — Always Tested!

Type I Error (α) = FALSE POSITIVE

You reject the null hypothesis when it is actually true. In other words, you conclude that a drug works when it really does not.

Type II Error (β) = FALSE NEGATIVE

You fail to reject the null hypothesis when it is actually false. In other words, you miss a real effect — you conclude the drug does not work when it actually does.

Power = 1 − β = the probability of correctly detecting a real effect.

Key relationships to remember:

- Increasing the sample size INCREASES power (reduces β).
- Z-alpha = 1.96 for a 95% confidence level.
- Z-beta = 0.84 for 80% power.
- Reducing α (being stricter about false positives) increases the chance of false negatives (β) — there is always a trade-off.

The 8-Step Process for Calculating Sample Size

Calculating sample size is not a single calculation — it is a structured process with eight steps. Skipping any step leads to an incorrect sample size.

Table 10.5: The 8-Step Sample Size Calculation Process

Step	What You Do and Why
Step 1	Identify the major study variable (your primary outcome). Sample size is calculated for the one most important variable in your study. Different variables may give different required sample sizes — you use the largest one.
Step 2	Determine the type of estimate you need. Are you estimating a mean (e.g., average blood pressure), a proportion (e.g., percentage vaccinated), a ratio, or a difference between two groups? The formula you use depends on this answer.
Step 3	Estimate the expected frequency or value from existing literature or pilot data. For example, if previous studies show that 40% of children in your area are malnourished, you use p = 0.40 in your formula. If no estimate exists, use p = 0.5.
Step 4	Decide on the desired precision (the 'd' value). Precision is how close your sample estimate needs to be to the true value. A precision of ±5% means you are willing to accept that your estimate might be up to 5% away from the truth in either direction.
Step 5	Set the acceptable risk levels (alpha and beta). Conventionally, α = 0.05 and β = 0.20, giving z_α = 1.96 and z_β = 0.84.

Step	What You Do and Why
Step 6	Apply the finite population correction if the population is small. If you are sampling from a small, well-defined group, your required sample size can actually be smaller than the formula suggests.
Step 7	Adjust for Design Effect if you are using cluster sampling. Multiply your calculated n by the design effect (DEFF), which is typically between 1.5 and 2.0. This corrects for the fact that cluster samples are less statistically efficient than simple random samples.
Step 8	Adjust for expected non-response. Divide the adjusted n by (1 − expected non-response rate). If you expect 20% of people to not respond or drop out, divide by 0.80. In practice, add 10–20% extra to your sample to buffer against dropout.

Sample Size Formulas with Worked Examples

Formula 1: Estimating a Mean

$$n = (z^2 \times \sigma^2) / d^2$$

Where z = z-alpha (1.96 for 95% CI), σ = the standard deviation of the outcome in the population, and d = the desired precision.

Worked Example: Protein Intake Survey

You want to estimate the average daily protein intake in a population. From previous studies, the standard deviation (σ) of protein intake is known to be 20 grams. You want your estimate to be within ±5 grams of the true value (d = 5). You choose a 95% confidence interval (z = 1.96).

$n = (1.96)^2 \times (20)^2 / (5)^2$

$n = 3.84 \times 400 / 25$

$n = 1536 / 25$

$n = 61.47$

Always round up to the next whole number. Therefore, n = 62 participants.

Formula 2: Estimating a Proportion

$n = (z^2 \times p \times q) / d^2$ where $q = 1 - p$

Where p = the expected proportion in the population, $q = 1 - p$, and d = the desired absolute precision.

Worked Example: Immunisation Coverage Survey

You want to estimate the immunisation coverage rate in a district. Previous data suggests coverage is approximately 80% ($p = 0.80$). You want your estimate to be within ±4% of the true value ($d = 0.04$). You choose a 95% confidence interval ($z = 1.96$).

$n = (1.96)^2 \times 0.80 \times 0.20 / (0.04)^2$

$n = 3.84 \times 0.16 / 0.0016$

$n = 0.6144 / 0.0016$

$n = 384$ participants

Important: If you have no estimate of p from the literature, use $p = 0.5$. This is because $p \times q$ is maximised when $p = 0.5$ (giving $0.5 \times 0.5 = 0.25$), which produces the largest — and therefore most conservative — sample size. This ensures you will not underestimate how many participants you need.

Important Adjustments to Sample Size

Table 10.6: Adjustments to Sample Size

Adjustment Type	When It Is Needed	How to Apply It
Design Effect (DEFF)	When you are using cluster or multistage sampling, which is less efficient than SRS.	Multiply your calculated n by the DEFF. A DEFF of 1.5 means you need 50% more participants than SRS would suggest.
Non-Response Adjustment	When you expect some participants to refuse, be unavailable, or drop out of the study.	Divide n by (1 − non-response rate). If 20% dropout is expected, divide n by 0.80.
Confounder Adjustment	When your analytical study involves multiple potential confounding variables that you plan to adjust for.	Add approximately 10% to your sample size for each confounding variable you plan to include in your analysis.
Finite Population Correction	When your population is small and you are sampling a substantial fraction of it.	Apply the finite population correction formula to reduce the required sample size.

Recommended Free Software for Sample Size Calculation

You do not always need to calculate sample size by hand. The following free tools are widely used and accepted:

- OpenEpi (www.openepi.com) — Supported by the CDC Atlanta. Handles multiple study designs including proportions, means, case-control studies, and cohort studies.
- PS (Power and Sample Size) — Developed by Vanderbilt University. Excellent for clinical trials and comparison studies.

Regardless of which tool you use, always report the software name, version number, and every input assumption (p, d, α, β, DEFF, non-response rate) in the Methods section of your paper. Other researchers must be able to reproduce your calculation.

10.6 Selecting the Study Population: From Everyone to Your Sample

One of the most conceptually important tasks in study design is understanding the relationship between different 'levels' of population, and being able to precisely define which population your study actually applies to.

There are four levels, arranged from largest to smallest:

Table 10.7: Levels of Study Population

Population Level	Defined By	Example: PCOS and Dysmenorrhoea Study
General Population	The entire community, country, or world.	All women in India.
Target Population	Clinical and demographic characteristics that are directly relevant to the research question.	Women aged 15–44 years who have both PCOS and dysmenorrhoea.
Accessible Population	A geographically and temporally defined subset of the target population — the people you can actually reach.	PCOS patients attending the outpatient department of the study hospital between January and December of the study year.
Study Sample	The actual participants enrolled in the study, selected from the accessible population using your sampling method.	n = 150 PCOS patients enrolled via systematic sampling.

Understanding these levels is important because the results of your study can only be directly generalised to the accessible population, and by extension (with appropriate caution) to the target population. They cannot automatically be extended to the entire general population.

Inclusion and Exclusion Criteria

Once you have defined your study population, you need to specify exactly who will be allowed into the study (inclusion criteria) and who will be kept out (exclusion criteria). These criteria must be defined before data collection begins, and they must be based on scientific reasoning — not convenience.

Table 10.8: Inclusion and Exclusion Criteria

Criteria Type	Purpose	Based On
Inclusion Criteria	Define the characteristics that every participant must have. These criteria ensure that enrolled subjects are genuinely relevant to your research question.	Clinical characteristics (e.g., confirmed diagnosis), demographic characteristics (e.g., age range), geographical characteristics (e.g., resident of study district), and temporal characteristics (e.g., attending clinic during study period).
Exclusion Criteria	Define the characteristics that would prevent a person from being included, even if they meet the inclusion criteria. These protect the quality, safety, and ethics of the study.	(1) High risk of being lost to follow-up (e.g., patient is about to relocate). (2) Potential to compromise data quality (e.g., unable to understand the questionnaire). (3) Ethical concerns (e.g., pregnant women in a drug trial). (4) Risk of adverse effects from the study procedures.

A common mistake is to make exclusion criteria too broad. Excluding too many people makes your sample less representative and limits the generalisability of your findings. Exclude only those who genuinely need to be excluded.

Key Takeaways — Chapter 10

1. Sampling is necessary because studying entire populations is usually not feasible. A well-chosen sample gives reliable, generalisable results at a fraction of the cost and time.

2. Probability sampling is the only method that allows valid statistical inferences to the population. Non-probability sampling is only suitable for hypothesis generation and exploratory work.

3. The five probability sampling methods are: Simple Random Sampling, Systematic, Stratified, Cluster, and Multistage. Each has specific use cases.

4. Cluster sampling introduces a Design Effect ($DEFF > 1$) because people within clusters are similar. Always multiply sample size by DEFF when using cluster sampling.

5. Type I Error (α) = false positive (concluding an effect exists when it does not). Type II Error (β) = false negative (missing a real effect). Power = $1 - \beta$.

6. When the expected proportion (p) is unknown, always use $p = 0.5$ — this gives the maximum (most conservative) sample size.

7. Target population is defined by clinical and demographic characteristics. Accessible population adds geographical and temporal restrictions.

8. Inclusion criteria define who must be included. Exclusion criteria define who must be kept out — and should be used sparingly to preserve generalisability.

9. Always adjust your final sample size for non-response (add 10–20% extra) and for design effect if applicable.

10. Internal validity (the study is measuring what it claims to measure, without bias) is always a prerequisite for external validity (the findings can be applied to the wider population).

Chapter 11: Planning Your Study — Study Design, Variables, Tools, and Protocol: Getting It Right Before You Begin

> *A researcher who designs a brilliant study but plans its execution poorly will end up with data that is impossible to analyse, results that are impossible to interpret, and interpretations that are useless for policy. Great research is not just good ideas — it is meticulous planning followed by disciplined execution.*

11.1 Why Good Planning Matters

Poor planning leads to a cascade of problems:

- Data that is difficult or impossible to analyse.
- Analysed data that is difficult to interpret correctly.
- Interpretations that are useless for informing policy or clinical practice.

The goal of project management is to ensure that defined objectives are adequately met within the defined time frame, with the available budget, without compromising data quality.

11.2 The Research Process Roadmap

Table 11.1: The Research Process Roadmap

Phase	Steps
Pre-Planning	1. Identify the research need 2. Verbalise and spell out the research question
Planning	3. Formulate study objectives 4. Plan the analysis 5. Prepare data collection instruments 6. Estimate sample size
Execution	7. Collect data 8. Analyse data
Dissemination	9. Draw appropriate conclusions 10. Make specific recommendations 11. Assess whether the original data need has been fulfilled

11.3 Formulating Study Objectives

A study with too many objectives is a confused study. The golden rule: FEWER IS BETTER. Long lists of objectives scatter attention and inflate your required sample size.

Table 11.2: Types of Study Objectives

Type	Purpose	Key Verb	Example
Primary Objective	Main question; DETERMINES the sample size for the entire study	'To determine...'	Determine whether a contaminated well caused the outbreak
Secondary Objective	Additional analysis; answerable from the same dataset	'To estimate...'	Estimate the prevalence of diabetes in the study population
Exploratory	Hypothesis generation from observed patterns	'To explore...'	Explore risk factors for childhood pneumonia
Confirmatory	Testing a known hypothesis with new data	'To confirm...' / 'To test...'	Test whether Vaccine X reduces disease incidence by 50%

11.4 Choosing the Right Study Design

Table 11.3: Matching Research Question to Study Design

Research Question	Best Design	Key Measure
Acute condition incidence (e.g., pneumonia)	Cohort or Surveillance study	Incidence rate
Chronic condition prevalence (e.g., diabetes)	Cross-sectional or Cohort study	Prevalence

Exposure → Outcome (frequent outcome, short lag)	Cohort study (prospective)	Relative Risk (RR)
Outcome → Exposure (rare disease, long lag)	Case-Control study (retrospective)	Odds Ratio (OR)
Quick snapshot of population	Cross-sectional analytical study	Prevalence, associations

11.5 Why Create an Analysis Plan BEFORE Collecting Data?

Many researchers think the analysis plan comes after data collection. This is backwards. Preparing the analysis plan — including empty (dummy) table shells — before starting has enormous benefits:

- Focuses attention firmly on the study objectives — you collect what you actually need.
- Prevents collecting enormous amounts of unnecessary data (and wasting everyone's time and money).
- Enables quicker publication — the analysis framework is already built.
- Prevents post hoc analysis — the cardinal sin of statistics (more on this in Chapter 12).

11.6 Why Studies Fail — and How to Prevent It

Table 11.4: Common Reasons for Study Failure and Prevention

Failure Reason	Prevention
Poorly defined research question or objectives	Invest time at the planning stage; consult the literature and experienced colleagues
Unrealistic time schedule	Develop a realistic Gantt chart; always pad timelines for contingencies
Inappropriate or incompetent staff	Careful recruitment; proper training; ongoing supervision
Lack of motivation or direction within the team	Regular team meetings; clear communication; strong leadership
Inadequate monitoring of data quality	Build a monitoring plan; assign supervisors with clear responsibilities
No response to contingencies that arise	Plan for mid-course corrections; always have backup plans for key processes

11.7 The Six Pillars of Successful Project Management

1. Human Resource Management

Carefully choose staff who match the skills required for the study type (clinical vs. field work). Train properly using a standardised protocol. Foster team communication through regular meetings. A study is only as strong as its weakest investigator.

2. Time Management

Schedule all activities; set clear milestones; ensure timely completion of each phase. The principal investigator is ultimately responsible for the timeline. Use a Gantt chart — a visual timeline that shows all activities and their overlap.

3. Financial Management

Plan fund releases in advance; meet deliverables to ensure continuous funding; avoid financial gaps that can stall data collection. Funding gaps are a common and devastating cause of study failure.

4. Quality Management

Maintain quality at every stage: data collection, clinical procedures, laboratory work, data management, and supervision. Quality cannot be retrospectively added — it must be built in from the start.

5. Data Management

This is perhaps the most neglected pillar. Conduct data management CONCURRENTLY in real time — do not leave it until the end. Errors detected early can be corrected. Errors detected after data collection is complete may be impossible to fix.

6. Monitoring and Supervision

Conduct internal or external monitoring throughout the study. Regular supervisory visits; mid-course corrections as soon as problems are identified. Never wait until the end of data collection to review how things are going.

11.8 Designing Data Collection Tools: The Questionnaire

A poorly designed data collection tool can single-handedly destroy an otherwise excellent study. Once data is collected with a flawed instrument, there is no going back. This point cannot be overstated.

Domains of Information to Collect

Table 11.5: Domains of Information in Data Collection

Domain	What It Covers
Facts	Characteristics of participants, their environment, and their behaviours or practices
Knowledge	Risk factor awareness; knowledge about disease prevention and healthy lifestyle
Judgements/Opinions	Attitudes toward health services; behaviours (e.g., seat belt use, open defecation)

Types of Data Collection Tools

Table 11.6: Types of Data Collection Tools

Tool	Description	Best Used For
Data Abstraction Form	Extracting information from existing records (clinical notes, registers, surveillance data)	Secondary data; disease history; treatment records
Structured Observation Checklist	Documenting whether processes are happening correctly and in sequence	Process evaluation; clinical procedure audits
Interviewer-Administered Questionnaire	Data collector asks questions face-to-face or by phone (CAPI = computer-assisted personal interviewing)	Complex questions; low-literacy populations; large surveys
Self-Administered Questionnaire	Respondent fills in the questionnaire directly (CASI = computer-assisted self-interview)	Literate populations; sensitive topics; large samples

Four Universal Components of Any Data Collection Tool

Table 11.7: Four Universal Components of a Data Collection Tool

Component	What It Contains
Introduction	Presents the study, states objectives, obtains informed consent
Identifiers	Name or address (on a separate sheet for confidentiality) OR coded composite ID numbers
Instructions	General prompts for data collectors; skip pattern instructions; use different fonts to distinguish from questions
Question Items	The body of the instrument — open, closed, or semi-open questions
Conclusion	Thank respondent; closing statement; instructions for returning the form

Types of Questions

Table 11.8: Types of Questions in a Questionnaire

Type	Description	Advantages	Disadvantages
Open Questions	Answer not suggested; respondent generates freely	Total freedom; stimulates memory;	Difficult to code and analyse; unfocused responses

		good for hypothesis generation	
Open Question with Closed Answers	Question is open but pre-coded categories exist (interviewer ticks without reading out)	Best of both worlds; analysed as closed data	Requires careful design of categories in advance
Closed — Dichotomous	Only two options (Yes/No, Male/Female)	Clear, focused; very easy to analyse	May oversimplify complex issues
Closed — Multiple options (single answer)	Multiple categories; only ONE acceptable answer	More nuanced than dichotomous	Must specify 'tick only one' clearly
Closed — Multiple options (multiple answers)	Multiple categories; MORE THAN ONE acceptable	Captures all relevant answers	Must specify 'tick all that apply'
Closed — Quantitative	Numeric answer required (e.g., age, number of clinic visits)	Creates continuous variables; flexible for later analysis	Some quantities are hard to interpret directly
Semi-open Questions	Closed categories PLUS an 'Other (specify)' option	Captures unexpected answers not covered by categories	Too many 'other' responses complicate analysis

Question Formulation: The Golden Rules

Table 11.9: Question Formulation: Do's and Don'ts

DO	DO NOT
Use short, precise, complete phrases (e.g., 'What is your age?' not just 'Age:')	Use negatives — especially double negatives
Use simple everyday language; avoid academic jargon	Ask leading or judgmental questions (e.g., avoid 'promiscuous' — use 'How many partners...')
Ask ONE question at a time — no double-barrelled questions	Combine two questions into one sentence
Use a neutral, non-judgmental tone throughout	Use vague language (e.g., avoid 'Do you eat healthily?' — it means nothing)
Be specific and unambiguous	Use technical terms a lay participant will not understand

Question Ordering Principles

- Start with SIMPLE questions; complex questions come later in the flow.
- Begin with GENERAL (demographic) questions, then move to SPECIFIC study questions.
- CASUAL and FACTUAL questions first; sensitive and attitudinal questions last.
- GROUP all questions on the same topic together — do not scatter them.
- Sequence of events should follow CHRONOLOGICAL order.
- Give the respondent a BREAK in the middle of a long questionnaire.
- The same topic asked multiple ways at different points = triangulation to verify response validity.

Questionnaire Layout Best Practices

- Use clear separators or lines between sections.
- Do NOT cramp questions — leave adequate space between them.
- Use 11–12 pt font for readability.
- Never split a question across two pages.
- Questions on the LEFT, answer codes on the RIGHT — neat two-column layout.
- Number ALL questions starting from 1.
- Build coding into the questionnaire from the start (e.g., Yes=1, No=0 consistently throughout).
- Auto-coding: number response categories 1, 2, 3, 4 — these become the data codes directly.

Pilot Testing and Finalisation

Why pilot test? To confirm questions are clear and understandable; check that questions are acceptable to respondents; verify that flow and skip patterns work; ensure coding works for data entry; and estimate the time required to complete the questionnaire.

Who should review the tool? Colleagues and subject matter experts; a statistician (to review coding and analysis compatibility); and field workers or data collectors (for practical flow and clarity).

Translation protocol: Translate from English to the local language. Then perform BACK-TRANSLATION — a different independent person translates the local language version back to English. Compare the original and back-translated versions for semantic equivalence. Any discrepancies must be resolved before use.

Critical Rule: Pilot test subjects must NOT be included in the main study.

Key Takeaways — Chapter 11

- Good planning prevents unusable data. Poor planning = wasted time, money, and effort.
- Primary objective determines the sample size for the entire study.
- Always prepare an analysis plan and dummy tables BEFORE collecting data.
- Six pillars: Human Resources, Time, Financial, Quality, Data Management, Monitoring.
- Concurrent data management is essential — errors caught in real time can be corrected.
- A data collection tool can make or break a study. Design it with extreme care.
- Always pilot test; always back-translate; pilot subjects are NOT included in the main study.
- One question at a time; no double negatives; no leading questions; build in coding from the start.

Chapter 12: From Field to Clean Dataset — Data Collection, Management, and Analysis: Executing, Storing, and Analysing Your Study Data

No one writes passionate journal articles about data management. Nobody delivers keynote lectures on how they cleaned their dataset. And yet, more studies have been ruined by poor data quality than by any flawed theoretical concept. Good data management is the invisible scaffolding that holds the entire research enterprise together.

12.1 The Two Foundations of Data Quality

Two fundamental attributes determine whether your research data is trustworthy:

Table 12.1: The Two Foundations of Data Quality

Attribute	Definition	Key Point
RELIABILITY	Repeatability and precision of measurement. The same result is obtained by different investigators, and the same result is obtained at different time points.	Reliability refers to STABILITY and CONSISTENCY. A reliable measure does NOT guarantee accuracy.
ACCURACY	The ability of a measurement to be correct — it measures what it is truly intended to measure.	Accuracy = validity of the measurement. An ideal study needs BOTH reliability AND accuracy.

Table 12.2: Reliability and Accuracy Scenarios

Scenario	Reliable?	Accurate?	Outcome
Ideal	Yes	Yes	Measurements are repeatable AND correct — best case scenario
Consistently wrong	Yes	No	Same wrong result every time — systematic bias
Correct but inconsistent	No	Yes	Correct on average but not reproducible
Worst case	No	No	Random errors everywhere — data is worthless

12.2 Six Principles of Data Collection

QTSR-DV — Six Principles of Data Collection

- Q = Question-by-Question Guide | T = Staff Training | S = Supervision
- R = Periodic Reviews | D = Debriefing | V = Data Validation

Principle 1: The Question-by-Question (Q-by-Q) Guide

A Q-by-Q guide is a short document that standardises data collection across all investigators. It is the road map that every investigator consults when in doubt about how to ask a question or record an answer.

- Contains a written explanation under each question describing exactly how to ask it and what responses to expect.
- Includes probes, skip patterns, and areas requiring extra emphasis or clarification.
- Ensures uniform interpretation by all investigators across all sites.
- Must be UPDATED and DOCUMENTED whenever field changes arise — any modification must be written in the Q-by-Q guide.

Principle 2: Staff Training

Table 12.3: Staff Training Steps for Data Collection

Step	Training Action
1	Select the RIGHT investigators — match skills to the study type (clinical vs. field)
2	Orientation: overview of the study, definitions, components, types of data to be collected
3	Walk through the Q-by-Q guide; discuss each question; allow investigators to ask questions

4	Classroom simulation: one investigator interviews another as a mock respondent
5	Pilot testing in a SIMILAR (not the same) setting before actual data collection begins
6	Clarify all doubts arising from the pilot; repeat until everyone is confident and consistent

Principle 3: Supervision

- Assign a supervisor who verifies completed forms EVERY DAY — not weekly.
- The supervisor identifies and corrects errors immediately, before leaving the site.
- The principal investigator should be reachable by phone for queries during data collection.
- The PI should conduct periodic on-site visits to verify protocol adherence.
- Never allow time pressure to compromise data quality — do not sacrifice quality for speed.

Principle 4: Periodic Reviews

- Hold regular meetings (weekly or monthly depending on study duration).
- Clarify questionnaire queries; resolve inconsistencies found in the field.
- Any changes made during reviews MUST be documented in the Q-by-Q guide.
- Allows early detection of systematic errors before they affect the whole dataset.

Principle 5: Periodic Debriefing

Field staff may encounter difficulties that were not anticipated during training. Provide a platform for team members to raise concerns, share experiences, and flag emerging problems. This is vital for team morale and for maintaining consistent data quality throughout the study.

Principle 6: Data Validation

Select a random sub-sample — as small as 5% is acceptable — and conduct an INDEPENDENT second interview on the same participants. Compare results from both interviews to detect discrepancies. Identify whether errors are due to individual investigators or are team-wide systematic errors. Address accordingly.

Field Quality Checks at the Form Level

Once completed forms are returned, apply three checks before entry:

Table 12.4: Field Quality Checks for Completed Forms

Check	What to Look For	Action
Completeness	Blank fields — unanswered or unrecorded questions	Return to investigator to fill or re-ask

Readability	Illegible handwriting; unclear narrative descriptions	Ask for re-writing or clarification
Consistency	Contradictory answers; biologically or logically implausible responses (e.g., a 2-year-old reporting employment)	Review with investigator; check for misunderstanding

12.3 Data Management: From Raw Data to Clean Dataset

Data management encompasses all steps from raw data entry to a clean, analysis-ready dataset. It is the bridge between data collection and data analysis.

Data management includes: defining variables and creating a data dictionary; creating and structuring the study database; entering data and correcting errors; creating an analysis-ready dataset; and backing up and archiving the dataset.

Data Documentation

Before any data entry begins, create a formal document that records all information about the database structure:

Table 12.5: Elements of Data Documentation

Element	Description
Structure	Name, number of records, and relevant structural information about the database
Variables	Variable names, assigned codes and values, and data types for each variable
History	When the database was created, modified, and by whom
Storage	Media used, backup locations, and archival procedures

Unique Identifier (UID)

Every participant record must have a Unique Identifier — a code distinct for each participant, maintained by a computerised index with quality assurance procedures that guarantee the internal validity of each record.

Example of a 7-digit UID structure: Digits 1–2 = Village or area code; Digits 3–4 = Street number; Digit 5 = House number; Digits 6–7 = Person's sequential number in the household.

Variable Specification and Naming Rules

Table 12.6: Variable Specification and Naming Rules

Variable Type	Specification Required
Numeric	Number of decimal places; permissible range (min–max)
Text / Alphanumeric	Field length; standardise all letters to CAPITALS to avoid errors
Date	Format: DD/MM/YYYY (India) vs. MM/DD/YYYY (USA) — specify upfront and stick to one format consistently
Coded values	What each code means (e.g., 1=Yes, 2=No, 9=Missing) — never leave this ambiguous

Variable naming rules: Names should be SELF-EXPLANATORY (clearly refer to the questionnaire item, e.g., EXERDAILY = exercise daily), SHORT (under 10 characters), have NO SPACES, and follow a CONSISTENT naming pattern (e.g., EXERPAST, EXERCURR, EXERDAILY). Always distinguish the crude variable (EXERCISE) from the recoded/derived version (EXERCISE_DIC = dichotomised version). It is best practice to assign variable names manually — avoid letting software auto-assign, as this can cause duplicates and confusion.

Coding Guidelines

- Prefer NUMERICAL coding for quantitative analysis.
- Missing values: use a dot (.) OR 999 — avoid using 99 for age, as it could be misread as a valid age value.
- Decide upfront: 1=Yes/0=No OR 1=Yes/2=No — and stick to it throughout the entire dataset.
- Avoid creating compound codes (e.g., '12' for walking + cycling) — this makes the variable unanalysable.

Database Design: Individual vs. Aggregated

Table 12.7: Individual vs. Aggregated Database Design

Database Type	Structure	Best For
Individual (Flat) Database	Each row = one participant; columns = individual variable values; one count per row per variable	Most epidemiological studies; individual-level analysis
Aggregated Database	Each row = a group or area (e.g., village); cells contain counts or frequencies	Ecological studies; surveillance; mapping

Mother and Daughter Databases

When data is collected at multiple hierarchical levels (e.g., village, household, individual, episode), use a mother-daughter database structure:

- Village-level database (mother) — contains village characteristics.
- Household-level database (daughter of village) — contains household variables.
- Individual-level database (daughter of household) — contains person-level data.
- Episode-level database (daughter of individual) — multiple illness episodes per person.

Linking rule: store data at the level where it belongs — do not repeat higher-level data in lower-level records. Link databases using a COMMON KEY (e.g., House ID links the household database to the individual database). Merge only at the time of analysis using software relational functions.

Important

- Avoid using spreadsheets (e.g., Excel) for data analysis. Use dedicated statistical software instead: EpiInfo (free; recommended for beginners), SPSS, Stata, or R.
- EpiInfo is particularly useful: it allows questionnaire design, data entry with validation checks, and statistical analysis all in one package.

12.4 Overview of Data Analysis: The Seven-Step Strategy

Data analysis is not something you improvise on the day. It is a structured process that follows the pre-specified analysis plan.

Table 12.8: The Seven-Step Data Analysis Strategy

Step	Action
Step 1: Identify study type	Is this a descriptive study (describe one group) or an analytical study (compare two or more groups)?
Step 2: Identify main variables	Outcome variable (dependent); exposure variable (independent); confounders/effect modifiers; subgroup variables
Step 3: Familiarise with the data	Frequencies; descriptive stats; check for duplicates; check for missing values; check ranges; check consistency
Step 4: Characterise the study population	Demographics; clinical features; compare baseline characteristics between groups — this becomes Table 1 in your paper
Step 5: Examine exposure-outcome association	Appropriate measure for study design (RR, OR, or PR); univariate then stratified then multivariate
Step 6: Create additional tables	New variables or cross-tabulations detected from initial findings
Step 7: Advanced analysis	Dose-response relationships; stratification; multivariate modelling

Measures of Association by Study Design

Table 12.9: Measures of Association by Study Design

Study Design	Outcome Type	Measure of Association
Cohort study	Acute or chronic disease	Relative Risk (RR) / Risk Ratio
Case-control study	Chronic or rare disease	Odds Ratio (OR)
Cross-sectional study	Prevalence-based	Prevalence Ratio (PR) or Prevalence Odds Ratio (POR)

Key Principle: Avoid Post Hoc Analysis

Post hoc analysis means generating a hypothesis FROM the data you are currently analysing, and then testing that hypothesis on the same data. This is a form of data dredging and is widely considered a serious methodological flaw.

The rule is simple: your analysis plan must be written BEFORE you start looking at your data, and you must stick to it. Exploratory analyses that generate new hypotheses are perfectly fine — but they must be clearly labelled as exploratory, and the new hypotheses must be tested in future studies with new data.

Key Takeaways — Chapter 12

- Reliability = repeatability. Accuracy = correctness. Both are needed for ideal data quality.
- Six principles: Q-by-Q guide, Training, Supervision, Reviews, Debriefing, Validation.
- Q-by-Q guide must be updated whenever field changes arise.
- Validation requires an INDEPENDENT interview on a sub-sample (minimum 5%).
- Data dictionary DESCRIBES variables. Database STORES data. They are different things.
- Missing value code: use 999 or dot (.). NEVER use 99 for age.
- Mother-daughter databases are linked by a common key — store data at the level where it belongs.
- Seven-step data analysis: Study Type → Variables → Familiarise → Characterise → Associate → Extra Tables → Advanced.
- Post hoc analysis must be avoided. Set your analysis plan before looking at the data.

Chapter 13: The Moral Compass — Research Ethics and Clinical Trial Conduct: Science Without Conscience Is Just Organised Curiosity

Between 1932 and 1972, the US Public Health Service conducted a study in Tuskegee, Alabama, in which 399 Black men with syphilis were denied effective treatment — even after penicillin became available — so that researchers could observe the natural progression of the disease. When the study was exposed, it shook the world's trust in medical research to its core. The ethical guidelines we follow today are built, in large part, on the ruins of that trust.

"Science is precise. Conscience is optional.

13.1 Why Ethics Review Is Non-Negotiable

Ethics review is mandatory for ALL health research — including studies using only existing data with no direct contact with participants. This requirement applies broadly. If human beings are involved in any way — even indirectly through their data — ethics review is required.

- Minimum risk studies (only questionnaires, no biological samples) also require ethics review.
- Both international standards AND Indian national standards (ICMR) must be followed.
- Ethics applies to research involving human participants, human biological material, or personal data.

13.2 Historical Timeline of Ethical Guidelines

Table 13.1: Historical Timeline of Research Ethics Guidelines

Year	Document / Event	Key Contribution
1947	Nuremberg Code	Post-WWII; established the requirement for voluntary consent; introduced risk-benefit analysis; required researcher competence
1964 (revised 2013)	Declaration of Helsinki	First major international consensus; individual rights; informed decisions; patient welfare; special protection for vulnerable groups
1978–79	Belmont Report (USA)	Defined the three core principles: Autonomy, Justice, Beneficence; established the Institutional Review Board (IRB); framework for informed consent
1992–93 (revised 2002)	CIOMS Guidelines (WHO)	Adverse event reporting; pharmacovigilance; continued safety surveillance after trials
1996	ICH-GCP Guidelines	Good Clinical Practice standards; applied to laboratory, epidemiological, and clinical research worldwide
2000 (revised 2006, 2017)	ICMR Ethical Guidelines (India)	National standards for all institutions conducting health research in India

13.3 Core Ethical Principles — The Belmont Report

Table 13.2: Core Ethical Principles — The Belmont Report

Principle	Meaning	Practical Implication
Autonomy	Respect for self-rule; respect human dignity and decision-making capacity	Participants have the RIGHT to choose whether to participate; no coercion; respect refusal
Justice	Treat all equally, fairly, and impartially; benefits of research extend to all	All groups (except those medically contraindicated) should have the opportunity to participate
Beneficence	Obligation to do good; maximise benefits to participants and the community	Research must provide benefit; investigators must actively promote participants' welfare
Non-maleficence	Do no harm; minimise risks to the greatest extent possible	Take all steps to minimise harm; if harm occurs, provide appropriate care and support

13.4 Informed Consent: A Process, Not a Form

Informed consent is a systematic, step-by-step process by which potential participants are empowered to make a voluntary, informed decision about research participation. It is not a one-time transaction — it is an ongoing relationship of trust and transparency.

Components of the Informed Consent Form

Table 13.3: Components of the Informed Consent Form

Section	Content
Header	Name of project and conducting agency
Study description	Brief, clear explanation of what the study involves; what participants will be asked to do
Risks	ALL potential risks explained honestly — physical, psychological, social, and financial
Benefits	Individual AND community benefits; it is acceptable if there is no direct personal benefit
Alternatives	Participant can decline; regular health services will continue regardless of participation
Confidentiality	Assurance that records will be kept confidential; explain how data will be stored and who can access it
Compensation clause	If harm results directly from participation, compensation will be provided
Contact information	Name and contact details of whom to approach for queries or concerns during the study
Voluntary participation	Explicit statement of the right to decline or withdraw at ANY time without penalty
Signature	Participant signs; if illiterate — an IMPARTIAL WITNESS (NOT from the study team) signs

Critical Rules for Informed Consent

- Must be in the LOCAL language; back-translated and verified for accuracy.
- Language must be SIMPLE and CLEAR — no medical jargon for lay participants.
- TWO copies signed: one kept by the participant, one with the investigator team.
- Group consent (in tribal or institutional settings) does NOT replace individual consent.
- Oral consent alone is generally NOT sufficient; written consent is required.
- Audio-visual recording is now MANDATORY for IND (Investigational New Drug) trials in India.
- A test of understanding may be administered to verify comprehension — this is good practice.
- The Principal Investigator CANNOT sign as an impartial witness — must be someone entirely unconnected to the study.

Exam Insight: Informed Consent Rules

- Informed consent is a PROCESS — may require multiple sittings.
- Group consent does NOT replace individual consent.
- Audio-visual recording mandatory for IND trials in India.

- PI cannot sign as impartial witness.
- Ethics review is required EVEN for studies using available data with NO direct risk.

13.5 Stakeholders in the Informed Consent Process

Table 13.4: Stakeholders in the Informed Consent Process

Stakeholder	Obligations
Investigators / Researchers	Provide complete, in-depth information; answer all questions honestly; ensure the decision is truly voluntary; document the entire consent process
Participants	Understand the information given; know their rights and provisions; sign freely without coercion; fulfil the obligations agreed to during the study
Sponsors / Monitors / Regulators	Assess fairness of the consenting process; verify consent documentation; monitor throughout the trial to ensure consent is maintained

13.6 Types of Review Required Before Research Begins

Table 13.5: Types of Review Required Before Research Begins

Step	Review Type	What Is Assessed
1	Scientific Review (by Institutional SAC)	Novelty; rationality; study design; methodology; sample size; clinical endpoints
2	Regulatory Review (CDSCO/GEAC/HMSC)	Drug or vaccine regulatory requirements; import regulations; genetic product approvals; international funding clearances
3	Ethical Review (IEC)	Safety and welfare of participants; competence of research team; protection of human rights; informed consent; adverse event management; confidentiality

Note: IEC in India = IRB (Institutional Review Board) in the Western context. They serve the same function.

13.7 Conducting Clinical Trials: Good Clinical Practice (GCP)

Good Clinical Practice (GCP) is an international standard for designing, conducting, recording, and reporting clinical trials. It ensures credibility and ethical conduct throughout the trial lifecycle.

Mandatory Approvals Before Starting a Clinical Trial

- Step 1: Scientific Review by Institutional Scientific Advisory Committee (ISAC).
- Step 2: Ethical Review by Institutional Ethics Committee (IEC) or National Ethics Committee.
- Step 3: Regulatory Review by CDSCO (formerly DCGI); HMSC for international funding; GEAC for GMO products.
- Step 4: Keep all approval certificates on file for external monitors and regulatory agencies.

GCP Core Requirements

- Enrol only participants who meet the exactly defined inclusion/exclusion criteria.
- Follow ALL study procedures EXACTLY as defined in the protocol — no improvisation.
- Collect biological samples exactly as specified (volume, timing, storage).
- Ensure ALL scheduled visits are completed by participants.
- Document everything; maintain complete, accurate, legible records at all times.
- Adhere to intervention (medication compliance) protocols.

Safety Monitoring and Adverse Events

Table 13.6: Safety Monitoring and Adverse Events in Trials

Term	Definition
Adverse Event (AE)	Any untoward medical occurrence in a trial participant — not necessarily causally related to the intervention
Serious Adverse Event (SAE)	Death, serious complication, OR hospitalisation for any cause during trial participation
DSMB	Data Safety Monitoring Board — an INDEPENDENT, pre-defined body that reviews safety data and decides whether the trial should continue

- All AEs must be documented — including laboratory abnormalities and social or familial problems.
- SAEs must be reported PROMPTLY to: regulatory authorities + sponsors + ethics committee.
- After 3 SAEs: DSMB reviews relatedness to the intervention and decides whether the trial should continue or stop.
- DSMB is INDEPENDENT — it cannot be influenced by sponsors or investigators.
- Trial stoppage rules (e.g., stop after any 3 SAEs) must be defined UPFRONT in the protocol.

Reimbursements vs. Incentives

Table 13.7: Reimbursements vs. Incentives in Research

Type	Description	Ethical Status
Reimbursement (Acceptable)	Compensation for time at site; lost daily wages; travel costs; food expenses during long visits. Should NOT exceed actual expenses.	Acceptable — covers genuine costs
Incentive (Use Caution)	Payment beyond actual expenses. Risk: if too large, could be COERCIVE — may induce participation against free choice.	Must be approved by Ethics Committee; recent government regulations specify limits

Key Takeaways — Chapter 13

- Ethics review is mandatory for ALL research — even studies using only existing data.
- Nuremberg Code (1947): voluntary consent. Helsinki (1964, revised 2013): individual rights. Belmont Report (1978–79): Autonomy, Justice, Beneficence.
- ICMR Ethical Guidelines (India): 2000, revised 2006 and 2017.
- Informed consent is a PROCESS, not a form. Group consent does NOT replace individual consent.
- IEC (India) = IRB (USA) — same function.
- Three sequential approvals for clinical trials: Scientific → Ethical → Regulatory.
- DSMB = independent body; decides trial continuation after SAEs.
- Reimbursement is acceptable; coercive incentives are not.
- GCP: enrol only eligible participants; follow protocol exactly; document everything.

Chapter 14: From Idea to Print — Concept Papers, Protocols, Ethics, Manuscripts, and Grants: The Long Journey from 'I Have an Idea' to 'It Is Published'

Every published paper that changes clinical practice, influences policy, or saves lives began as a vague idea in someone's head. Between that vague idea and a published paper lies a long, structured journey — concept paper, protocol, ethics approval, data collection, analysis, writing, peer review, and revision. This chapter covers that entire journey, from the one-page concept paper all the way to the grant proposal that funds the next cycle.

14.1 The Concept Paper: Getting the Idea onto Paper

A concept paper is a one-page miniature protocol — the very first step in transforming a research idea into a funded study. ICMR calls it a 'pre-proposal'. Its purpose is to FORCE you to think through your idea clearly enough to write it down in one page. This act alone filters out half the ideas that would never have worked anyway.

One-page format matters because:

- It forces focus and overcomes writing inhibition — ideas get born rather than staying as mere thoughts.
- It is required by most funding agencies as a pre-proposal before a full submission.
- ICMR STS (Short-Term Studentship) proposals for medical undergraduates follow exactly this structure.

7 Steps of a Successful Protocol Development

Table 14.1: Seven Steps of Successful Protocol Development

Step	Action
Step 1	Identify the research topic
Step 2	Frame the research question and objectives
Step 3	Outline a one-page concept paper
Step 4	Prepare dummy tables (the analysis plan)
Step 5	Write a detailed draft protocol
Step 6	Prepare instruments and annexures (information sheet, consent form, questionnaire)
Step 7	Submit to peer review committee and the ethics committee

The Six Sections of a Concept Paper

Table 14.2: The Six Sections of a Concept Paper

Sections of a Concept Paper

- B = Background & Justification
- O = Objectives (max 2–3; clearly primary vs. secondary)
- M = Methods (design, population, definitions, sampling, sample size, data collection, analysis plan, ethical issues)
- E = Expected Benefits
- R = References (max 5; ICMJE citation format)
- B = Budget (indicative only)

Section	Content and Tips
Background & Justification	3 bullets: (1) Importance of study problem with quantification, (2) What is known and unknown locally, (3) Information needed to address the problem
Statement of Objectives	Max 2–3 objectives; clearly distinguish primary vs. secondary; state quantitatively where possible

Methods	Study design; study population; key operational definitions; sampling; sample size; data collection (who collects what, when, and how); analysis plan; ethical issues
Expected Benefits	(1) What action or policy change follows from the results? (2) What future research or policy agenda does this open up?
Key References	Maximum 5 references; follow ICMJE guidelines for citation format
Budget	Indicative only; cover: salaries/per diem, travel, equipment/supplies, miscellaneous

14.2 The Research Protocol: Expanding the Idea

A research protocol is the full written plan for a study — all the structural elements of the research project combined in a formal, detailed written format. It expands the concept paper's bullet points into full paragraphs.

- First draft: 1,500–2,000 words; the introduction should not exceed one-fifth of the total length.
- Start with the concept paper as your outline, then expand each bullet point into a paragraph.
- References increase from 5 (concept paper) to 5–10 or more.
- Multiple drafts are normal; archive every draft.

Elements of the Methods Section

Table 14.3: Elements of the Methods Section in a Protocol

Protocol Methods Sections

- D = Study Design | I = Interventions (if applicable) | O = Operational Definitions
- D = Demographics / Study Population | S = Sampling | S = Sample Size
- D = Data Collection | A = Analysis Plan | I = Implementation Plan + Timeline | H = Human Subject Protection

Section	What to Include
Study Design	Explain how objectives will be measured; define indicators; state design type (experimental or observational: cohort, case-control, cross-sectional); specify prospective vs. retrospective
Interventions (if applicable)	Only for experimental studies; describe WHO is intervened, WHAT the intervention is, time period, and full procedure
Operational Definitions	Define and measure key outcome and exposure variables; use standard validated definitions with references; be precise and unambiguous

Study Population	Inclusion AND exclusion criteria; time period; geographical location; individual characteristics. Note: study population differs from study sample
Sampling	Type of sampling (random or non-random); all steps; references for standard methods; for RCTs: randomisation technique and allocation to arms
Sample Size	Parameters used; formula applied; software used; references; depends on study objective AND sampling methodology
Data Collection	WHAT data (sociodemographic, clinical, lab); WHO collects it (PI, nurse, field worker); HOW (interview, observation, abstraction, lab assay)
Analysis Plan	Mode of data entry; software; recoding variables; parameters to estimate; steps of analysis for each objective. Avoid writing 'suitable analysis will be carried out' — this is not acceptable in a protocol.
Implementation Plan	Roles and responsibilities; timeline for each phase (designing instruments, ethics approval, pilot, data collection, entry, analysis, reporting)
Human Subjects Protection	Risks to participants; how risks will be minimised; benefits; informed consent details; ethics committee approval procedures

Key Reporting Guidelines

Table 14.4: Key Reporting Guidelines

Guideline	Study Type
STROBE	Strengthening the Reporting of Observational Studies in Epidemiology — for observational studies
CONSORT	Consolidated Standards of Reporting Trials — for randomised controlled trials
PRISMA	Preferred Reporting Items for Systematic Reviews and Meta-Analyses
SPIRIT	Standard Protocol Items for Randomised Trials — for clinical trial protocols

All reporting guidelines are available at: equator-network.org

14.3 Publication Ethics: The Five Commandments

1. Ethics Review and Breach of Confidentiality

- Obtain human or animal ethics committee approval BEFORE research begins — not after.

- Take informed consent (or age-appropriate assent) from all participants.
- Register clinical trials with the Clinical Trials Registry of India (CTRI) before recruitment begins.
- Do NOT share data outside your institution without institutional permission.
- Sharing unpublished data with others — even friends or colleagues — without permission is UNETHICAL.

2. Fabrication and Falsification

Term	Definition
Fabrication	Research results NOT generated from an actual study — data invented without doing the study at all
Falsification	Results generated by MANIPULATING existing data — changing data to produce desired results

- Both are extremely serious research misconduct — they undermine the entire foundation of scientific knowledge.
- Preserve data for a sufficiently long duration (paper or electronic) to defend against scrutiny.
- Make your analysis plan DURING study design; maintain it; report results exactly as found.

3. Authorship — ICMJE Criteria

Authorship is not a gift or an honour. It implies responsibility and accountability. All four ICMJE criteria must be met to qualify as an author:

- Substantial contribution to conception or design, OR to acquisition, analysis, or interpretation of data.
- Drafting the work OR revising it critically for important intellectual content.
- Final approval of the version to be published.
- Agreement to be accountable for all aspects of the work — accuracy and integrity.
- Decide authorship while writing the protocol itself — resolves ambiguity before it becomes conflict.
- Declare the contribution of each author — this is now mandatory for journal submission.

4. Plagiarism

Type	Definition
Plagiarism	Use of previously published work, OR unreferenced use of others' published or unpublished ideas, without consent, credit, or acknowledgement

Direct Plagiarism	Copying word-for-word from someone else's work
Self-Plagiarism	Duplicating your own previously published paper (also called duplicate publication)
Salami Publication	Publishing the same objective, hypothesis, and methodology as multiple separate papers — redundant publication that inflates the literature without adding knowledge

How to avoid plagiarism: write concepts in your own words; acknowledge ALL original sources including unpublished work; cite references accurately; avoid salami publications; use anti-plagiarism tools: Turnitin, iThenticate, URKUND (as per university norms).

5. Submission Ethics and Conflict of Interest

Issue	Definition
Simultaneous Submission	Submitting the same manuscript to different journals at the same time — NOT allowed
Duplicate Submission	Submitting a manuscript with the same hypothesis, methods, and data as an already-published paper — NOT allowed
Predatory Journals	Journals that do not properly peer review; listed by UGC-CARE (Consortium for Academic and Research Ethics)
Conflict of Interest (COI)	Financial, personal, social, or other interests that directly or indirectly influence the author's conduct. MUST be disclosed during manuscript submission.

Consequences of research misconduct: author can be blacklisted by all member journals of COPE (Committee on Publication Ethics); institution informed; institutional action taken.

14.4 Writing the Manuscript: The IMRD Structure

A manuscript is any document submitted for publication. Scientific manuscripts can be: original research, review of literature, correspondence, perspective, or editorial. All original research manuscripts follow the IMRD framework.

Table 14.5: Structure of a Scientific Manuscript (IMRD)

Section	Key Question	What to Include
Introduction (I)	WHY did you start?	Background of the research area; identified knowledge gaps; rationale of the project; specific objectives the project seeks to answer
Methods (M)	WHAT did you do?	Study setting; study design; operational definitions; sampling strategy and sample size; study procedures; data management; ethical principles

Results (R)	WHAT did you find?	Facts only — no interpretation or commentary; combination of text, tables, figures; do not repeat the same information in multiple formats
Discussion (D)	WHAT does it mean?	Summary of key findings (max 3 lines); interpretations; comparison with literature; strengths; limitations; conclusions; recommendations

The Discussion Section in Detail

The discussion requires the most intellectual investment of all sections. Here is the correct sequence:

- Summary of key findings — maximum 3 lines; what did you find?
- Interpretations and inferences from your results — what do your findings mean?
- Comparison with existing literature — balance between your own interpretations and the literature.
- Strengths of the study — novel design, methodology, setting, or population.
- Limitations — be honest; explain how each limitation might affect the results.
- Conclusions — ONE key take-home finding; must match a primary objective.
- Recommendations — for policy makers, clinicians, or practitioners.

Common Mistake: Concluding something that was not discussed in the article, or that is not supported by the primary results. Conclusions must flow directly from specific findings tied to primary objectives.

The Abstract: The Most Read Section

The abstract is the most commonly read — and most commonly written last but thought about least — part of any paper. Invest maximum time and thought in writing it.

- Length: 100–350 words.
- Structure: Background, Methods, Results, Conclusions (format varies by journal).
- Often required as a 'plain language summary' for general public readership.
- Write it last, after all other sections are complete.

The 6 S's of Scientific Writing

Table 14.6: The 6 S's of Scientific Writing

S	What It Means
Simple	Use everyday language; avoid jargon where possible
Short	Concise sentences; no redundant words or padding
Structured	Follow IMRD; use the argument matrix to trace each central idea through all sections

Sequential	Logical flow from one idea to the next; no sudden topic jumps
Strong	Evidence-based, confident statements; avoid vague hedging
Specific	Precise words; consistent terminology throughout; avoid ambiguity

The argument matrix: identify 2–3 central ideas or key messages. For each one, trace how it appears in the Introduction (as a gap), Methods (how you addressed it), Results (what you found), and Discussion (what it means). This ensures all sections are coherent.

14.5 Grant Proposal Writing: Funding Your Research

A grant proposal is a request for funding to conduct research. This is an essential career skill for researchers, and the sooner it is learned, the better. Most researchers maintain a generic proposal template and modify it for each specific funding call.

Elements of a Strong Grant Proposal

Table 14.7: Elements of a Strong Grant Proposal

Section	Key Points
Cover Letter	Brief, professional introduction to the funding body
Title Page	Project title, investigators, institutions, proposed dates
Abstract	Concise summary of the entire proposal
Introduction	Solid rationale; identify knowledge gap; state novelty clearly
Literature Review	Comprehensive but focused — justifies why the project is needed
Project Description	Objectives, study design, methodology — same as protocol methods
Budget & Justification	UNIQUE to grant proposals — the most critical section (see below)
Timeline	Gantt chart or activity table with dates
References	Key, relevant, recent; follow required citation style

The Budget: The Most Critical Section in a Grant Proposal

The budget section is unique to grant proposals. Always read the funding agency's guidelines BEFORE preparing the budget. Every item must be justified.

Category	Sub-category	Examples
Recurring Cost	Staff / Personnel	Scientists, field workers, data entry operators, nurses, lab technicians
Recurring Cost	Consumables	Syringes, printer ink, paper, gloves, stationery, files, reagents

Non-Recurring Cost	Equipment	Laptops, lab equipment, workstation furniture, software licences
Other Costs	Travel	Field visits, conference travel, site monitoring visits
Other Costs	Overhead Charges	2–5% of total project cost for space, electricity, telephone, vehicle use

Types of Funding Agencies

Table 14.8: Types of Funding Agencies

Type	Examples
Government (India)	ICMR (Indian Council of Medical Research), DST (Dept. of Science & Technology), DBT (Dept. of Biotechnology)
International	WHO, Wellcome Trust, Gates Foundation, NIH, USAID — require HMSC (Health Ministry Screening Committee) clearance for Indian researchers
Private / NGO	Reputable private organisations and non-governmental organisations

ICMR Grants: extramural grants for researchers in universities, medical colleges, and recognised labs; grants for PG/super-specialty thesis; grants for postdoctoral research; grants for international travel and research workshops. Note: ICMR grants are for researchers NOT employed by ICMR itself.

Factors That Increase Chances of Funding

- Read the funding call THOROUGHLY and strictly follow all guidelines — a technically non-compliant proposal is rejected before it is even read.
- Call the funding agency to clarify doubts in the application process.
- Be REALISTIC — do not undersell or oversell yourself.
- Study successful proposals from seniors and mentors.
- Build a collaborative, multi-disciplinary team (basic scientist, statistician, social scientist, economist).
- Build a track record before applying for large grants.
- Start early; leave time for feedback and revisions from multiple experts.
- Make EXPLICIT connections between all parts of the proposal.
- Highlight societal benefit and impact on vulnerable populations.
- Show institutional resource commitment through zero-cost items.

Key Takeaways — Chapter 14

- Concept paper = 1 page; 6 sections (B-O-M-E-R-B); max 5 references; indicative budget.
- Protocol methods: 10 paragraphs (D-I-O-D-S-S-D-A-I-H). Avoid writing 'suitable analysis will be carried out'.
- Fabrication = making up data. Falsification = manipulating data. Both are research misconduct.
- ICMJE authorship: ALL four criteria must be met. Decide authorship at the protocol stage.
- Salami publication = splitting one study into multiple papers = misconduct.
- IMRD structure: Introduction (Why?), Methods (What did you do?), Results (Facts only!), Discussion (What does it mean?).
- The abstract is the most commonly read section — invest maximum thought.
- Results section = Facts only. No interpretation. Save that for Discussion.
- Grant proposals are unique in requiring a detailed, justified budget.
- Even the most appealing proposal fails if sent to the wrong agency.

Final Recap: Everything You Need to Remember

Consider this your pre-exam companion — everything important, in one place, without the padding.

Master Summary: All Study Designs

Table FR.1: Master Summary of All Study Designs

Design	Direction	Measure	Best For	Main Limitation
Case Report	N/A	Descriptive	Rare/new manifestations; hypothesis generation	No comparison; no generalisability
Case Series	N/A	Descriptive	Characterise disease picture	No comparison group
Ecological	N/A	Group rates	Population-level hypotheses	Ecological fallacy
Cross-Sectional	Simultaneous	Prevalence	Quick burden measurement; service planning	No temporality
Cohort (Prospective)	Exposure → Outcome	RR + Incidence	Rare exposures; temporality; multiple outcomes	Expensive; long duration
Cohort (Retrospective)	Exposure → Outcome	RR + Incidence	Faster; uses existing records	Bias risk from records
Case-Control	Outcome → Exposure	Odds Ratio	Rare diseases; long-latency conditions	Recall bias; no incidence
RCT	Exposure → Outcome	RR / NNT	Efficacy testing; controlling confounding	Expensive; ethical challenges

High-Yield Quick-Fire Facts

Table FR.2: High-Yield Quick-Fire Facts

Fact	Answer
Bench to bedside	= Translational Research
Ethics review protects	Human participants
Regulatory review protects	Intellectual property and national interests

Random error — reduce by	Increasing sample size
Bias — reduce by	Improving study design
Confounder — control by	Statistical adjustment; restriction; matching; randomisation
Hypothesis required for	Analytical questions only (those with comparison groups)
Descriptive objective verb	To estimate
Analytical objective verb	To determine
Never use as objective verb	To study (too vague)
PubMed	25M+ citations; free; maintained by NLM/NIH
MeSH	Medical Subject Headings; NLM controlled vocabulary for searches
Boolean AND	Narrows the search
Boolean OR	Broadens the search
Boolean NOT	Excludes a term
P = I × D	Prevalence = Incidence x Duration
Diabetes mellitus	High prevalence + low incidence (chronic, long duration)
Common cold	Low prevalence + high incidence (short duration, resolves quickly)
Case fatality	Severity of disease — a proportion, not truly a rate
Cross-sectional limitation	Cannot establish temporality (chicken-and-egg problem)
PCP in 5 gay men (1981)	Classic case series → discovery of AIDS
Ecological fallacy	Group-level associations cannot be assumed for individuals
Cohort measures	Relative Risk (RR)
Case-control measures	Odds Ratio (OR)
OR formula	OR = ad/bc (cross-product ratio)
Framingham Heart Study	Classic prospective cohort study (CV risk factors)
Doll and Hill	Classic case-control study (smoking and lung cancer)
Case-control — prefer	INCIDENT cases over prevalent cases
Recall bias	Major weakness of case-control studies

Clinical trials	Gold standard; investigator manipulates the exposure
Phase I	Safety; <50 healthy volunteers
Phase II	Dose + safety; 100–500
Phase III	Efficacy; thousands; basis for regulatory approval
Phase IV	Post-marketing surveillance; rare adverse events
Randomisation controls	BOTH known AND unknown confounders
Triple-blind	Patient + investigator + analyst blinded
Internal validity	Accuracy within the study; prerequisite for generalisability
Grounded theory	Inductive; data → theory
Content analysis	Deductive; theory → data
FGD size	6–8 homogeneous participants
Type I Error (alpha)	False positive; rejecting a true null hypothesis
Type II Error (beta)	False negative; missing a real effect
Power	= 1 - beta; increased by larger sample size
p = 0.5	Gives maximum (most conservative) sample size for proportion estimation
Z-alpha (95% CI)	1.96
Z-beta (80% power)	0.84
Design Effect (DEFF)	Adjustment for cluster sampling; multiply n by DEFF (usually 1.5–2.0)
Target population	Defined by clinical + demographic characteristics
Accessible population	Defined by geographical + temporal characteristics
Reliability	Repeatability and consistency of measurement
Accuracy	Correctness of measurement (validity of the measure)
Q-by-Q guide	Standardises data collection; must be updated when field changes arise
Data validation	Independent re-interview of a sub-sample (minimum 5%)
Data dictionary	Describes variables — DIFFERENT from the database (which stores data)
Missing value code	Use 999 or dot (.). Avoid using 99 for age

Fabrication	Making up data without doing the study
Falsification	Manipulating existing data to produce desired results
ICMJE authorship	ALL four criteria must be met
Salami publication	Same work published as multiple papers = misconduct
Abstract	Most commonly read section; invest maximum thought
Results section	Facts only — no interpretation, no comparison with literature
Informed consent	A PROCESS, not just a form; must be in local language
Group consent	Does NOT replace individual consent
Nuremberg Code	1947; first document requiring voluntary consent
Helsinki Declaration	1964 (revised 2013); individual rights; vulnerable group protection
Belmont Report	1978–79 (USA); Autonomy, Justice, Beneficence; established IRBs
ICMR Guidelines India	2000; revised 2006 and 2017
IEC (India)	= IRB (USA/West) — same function, different name
DSMB	Data Safety Monitoring Board; independent; decides trial continuation after SAEs
CDSCO	Central Drugs Standard Control Organisation; drug regulatory authority in India
Never use for analysis	Spreadsheets (Excel) — use dedicated statistical software
Post hoc analysis	Generating hypotheses from the same data being analysed — must be avoided
STROBE	Reporting guideline for observational studies
CONSORT	Reporting guideline for randomised controlled trials
SPIRIT	Protocol guideline for randomised trials
PRISMA	Reporting guideline for systematic reviews and meta-analyses

A Final Word

Research is not just an academic exercise. Every well-designed, ethically conducted, carefully published study moves the needle on human health — sometimes by a millimetre, sometimes by a mile. John Snow removed a pump handle. Doll and Hill changed how the world thought about smoking. The teams behind every vaccine in your immunisation schedule ran clinical trials exactly like the ones described in this book.

You are not just studying for an exam. You are learning the language of evidence. Use it well.

About the Author

Dr Javed Ali completed his MBBS from PGIMS Rohtak. He has a keen interest in policy design, policy analysis, and research, with a focus on biomedical and public health domains.

His work reflects a deep commitment to making complex research methods accessible to students and early-career researchers — which is precisely why this book exists.

www.ingramcontent.com/pod-product-compliance
Lightning Source LLC
Chambersburg PA
CBHW080217170726
48282CB00030B/1148
* 9 7 8 9 3 5 8 1 0 0 2 5 9 *